IN THE MOOD

The Kings of the Big Bands

Colin King

Acknowledgments:
Courtesy of Redferns Music Picture Library:
p. 7, 78, 87, 102-103, 114-115 and 116 (Glen A. Baker); p. 11, 12-13, 14, 16-17, 24, 25, 40, 45 46-47, 49, 50, 58-59, 74 and 98 (Max Jones Files); p. 22, 26-27, 30-31, 33, 34, 37, 38, 52-53, 57, 61, 63, 65, 67, 69, 70, 73, 75, 76, 80, 83, 84, 90-91, 96 and 123 (Michael Ochs Archive); p. 43 (Jon Wilton); p. 55 (William P. Gottlieb); p. 89 (Leon Morris); p. 95 and 118-119 (David Redfern); p. 108 (RB); p. 113 and 124 (Bob Willoughby).

Published in 2002 by Caxton Editions
20 Bloomsbury Street
London WC1B 3JH
a member of the Caxton Publishing Group

Designed and produced for Caxton Editions
by Open Door Limited
Langham, Rutland
Editing: Mary Morton
Setting: Jane Booth
Colour separation: GA Graphics, Stamford, UK

Title: In the Mood, The Kings of Swing
ISBN: 1 84067 472 5

IN THE MOOD

The Kings of the Big Bands

Colin King

CAXTON EDITIONS

CONTENTS

INTRODUCTION

Nowadays, the musical term "swing" evokes a certain era, that of America in 1935–1945. It's a period now imbued with much nostalgia and inextricably linked to a style of dance, band arrangements and performance using rhythmic "riffs".

From before World War 1 and well into the 1920s, the more common forms of jazz music performance included Dixieland, hotel room and concert bands. The style of all these groups was distinguished by "ensemble" playing. During the 1930s, the music we now call "swing", developed out of this earlier ensemble style. Swing was a dense, rhythm-driven sound, almost always using a hard-driving "riff" against which the melody could be played. The swing style reached the peak of its popularity during the 1940s but remains a significant force to this day.

Two forms of swing evolved simultaneously: swing recordings and swing bands on radio. The arrangements used on the then still-new medium of records, consisted of tightly written, three-minute arrangements because that was the time limit allowed on the old 78 RPM records; after three minutes, the stylus hit the spindle. The swing music heard in live performances at dances and on the radio featured open-ended arrangements that allowed for longer improvisations by the musicians.

The swing sound was also defined by the band instrumentation. The older tenor reed-based sounds belonged to the 1920s dance bands and smaller "hot jazz" ensembles. But they evolved into larger bands, often of 16 pieces or more, where the brass section, trumpets and trombone, added their brighter, louder sound. The brass was counter-balanced by a bank of reeds, saxophones and clarinets. The rhythm was carried by piano, expanded drum set and guitar, while a string bass replaced the older tuba bass.

With the benefit of records and radio shows, the new bandleaders became heroes to a loyal following of admirers. Audiences would follow the adventures of their favourite band in newspapers and magazines. Some bands took up residence in the larger hotel lounges and ballrooms, broadcasting from those locations on national network radio. Other bands would constantly tour on a round of performances at country clubs, restaurants, concerts, and American college campuses.

Above: The swing music heard in live performances at dances and on the radio featured open-ended arrangements that allowed for longer improvisations by the musicians.

With the advent of swing, the role of the bandleader also changed. Some of the older leaders, men such as Paul Whiteman and Paul Ash who stood in front of a band and waved a baton, were replaced by bandleaders who were great instrumentalists in their own right. Men such as Benny Goodman, Glenn Miller, Tommy Dorsey and Artie Shaw would alternate between leading and soloing on each tune played. Other leaders led by playing piano full-time on each song. Among these were Count Basie and Duke Ellington.

Concurrent with that, the "sidemen" were given more opportunities to solo during the song. This caused a 'cult' following to develop for the best sidemen. Musicians like Gene Krupa gained their initial fame in this manner, often going on to become bandleaders in their own right. All of the bandsmen were becoming more visible and often the entire band would sing or "scat" an entire chorus (such as Johnny Long's 'Shanty in Old Shanty Town'). This was in keeping with the Southern American tradition of call and response.

"True music must repeat the thought and inspirations of the people and the time.
My people are Americans and my time is today."

GEORGE GERSHWIN

The music also began to vary. Ballads became much slower, more sentimental, while the faster music, tunes such as 'Opus One' and others, became almost frantic. The two types were often played alternately in the ballrooms and dance halls. A fast "jump" tune would be followed by a slow ballad giving the dancers a respite from doing the "Lindy Hop". During World War II, the slow ballads were extremely popular, especially between couples whose men were on leave from the battlefields. The recording industry became aware of what bandleader Kay Kaiser dubbed "GI nostalgia", that special longing for home and the sweetheart left behind.

Various piano styles were also popular during the swing period including Boogie Woogie, Stride, and Fast Western, also called Barrelhouse. The tunes were usually played by the smaller ensembles, and soloists.

It is very fair to say that swing truly dominated the social milieu. Swing music became the accompaniment at every kind of event – New York's swankiest night clubs, school proms, "juke joints" and even Young Communist League parties. Every section of society found some form of swing suitable for their purposes. Country club couples fox-trotted to 'Moonlight Serenade'; college students did 'The Big Apple' as a circle dance; and Harlem ballrooms exploded to the aerial acrobatics of the Savoy Swingers and the Audobon (Ballroom) Lindy-Hoppers.

Unfortunately, racism and segregation were prevalent. Just a few bands, the first of which was Benny Goodman's, followed by some of those formed by men who became famous working with Benny, such as Gene Krupa, Lionel Hampton and Teddy Wilson, were mixed groups. Admission and seating in theatres and

clubs throughout the country, and particularly in the South, was often restricted, and ensembles and audiences often segregated. Hollywood also had to handle swing bands on film with ingenuity. By interpolating swing ensembles into country-club or night-club settings, performances by black groups such as Duke Ellington, Louis Jordan and Chick Webb, could easily be edited out of the feature film for distribution in the Southern states, or these sequences could be lifted out and presented separately as independent short subject features.

Swing music's popularity reached its apogee throughout the late 1930s and the 1940s. America maintained swing's popularity throughout the World War II years when large and small ensembles toured army and navy camps both in the USA and abroad under the aegis of the USO and the War Manpower Commission Program. Especially on the warfronts, the servicemen's nostalgia for normality and home, and the effects of wartime stress, were eased by the live performances of touring bands as well as the special radio shows broadcast to the armed forces. Big band culture had by now become global.

Above: Various piano styles were also popular during the swing period including Boogie Woogie, Stride, and Fast Western, also called Barrelhouse.

EBONY AND IVORY

THE EARLY ORIGINS OF THE BIG BANDS

Before the 1880s, composers would write a melody, which in time would be orchestrated for a small orchestra. Bands would always play the tune the same way – precisely as it was orchestrated. Eventually, small groups of musicians took it upon themselves to improvise on the melody – to "jazz" it up. Early bands were usually very small groups, a frontline of cornet, trombone and clarinet/saxophone, and a backline (rhythm section) of brass bass (tuba), banjo (an American invention), drums and piano.

"If it hadn't been for jazz, there wouldn't be no rock and roll."

LOUIS ARMSTRONG

In the South, these bands would play "ensemble style", that is with no solos, with different instruments of the frontline varying, "Jazzing", the melody, while the musicians all played together (no solos). This "ensemble playing", with each instrument "jazzing up" its own part, is what came to be called Dixieland jazz.

When the music moved to S. Louis, Detroit and Chicago, it changed somewhat, most notably in two ways. Firstly, owing to the influence of one musician, Bix Beiderbecke, instrumental soloing became a feature of Dixieland jazz. Musicians, such as Louis Armstrong and others, would take Bix's idea and expand on it by making solos a fixed feature, along with routining the way bands would play, and some other improvements. Secondly, Dixieland changed into a harder driving form. In America's South, the music seemingly unfurled in front of you giving a relatively gentle sound.

Above: "Jazzing up" ensemble style.

NEW ORLEANS

I n the late-19th century New Orleans was two cities. There was the uptown, or American section, west of Canal Street, and the downtown, or French section, east of Canal Street. The downtown city had whites and Creoles, while uptown comprised the blacks who had only recently been freed from slavery. The Creoles were musically trained and the blacks, from uptown, often studied music with Creole instructors.

In 1894, all that changed as very restrictive racial segregation laws were promulgated, ensuring the segregation of even the Creoles. At first it was regarded as something of a comedown for the well-trained Creole musicians to be thrown into competition with the poorer, largely untrained uptown blacks, in order to play for audiences who rarely appreciated their "superior musical background". Fortunately, some years late, Creoles did collaborate with the uptowners, and added their own very special ethnic influences to the music. Men such as John Robichaux and Peter Bocage contributed a French-Haitian mixture; Alcibiades Jeanjacque, Oscar Duconge, Punkie and Bouboul Valentin lent their French style; while Lorenzo Tio, who had been educated at a Mexican conservatory, added a Spanish touch. The first blending and refining of jazz was already taking place. Musicians began to play what they felt and what their talents allowed, with each making his or her individual contribution to the whole.

In 1897, the city council passed legislation that restricted all prostitutes and brothels to a 38- square block area that came to be known as the Storyville district, or just "the district" to the locals. There were

even two Storyvilles – uptown side, "Back O' Town", west of Canal Street, was for blacks, while the downtown side, east of Canal Street, was for whites. At Storyville's peak, there were about 2,000 prostitutes plying their trade in various bagnios. These brothels employed every type of musician and musical group – ragtime pianists, string trios and even brass bands.

Above: The Storyville district in New Orleans.

Above: Kid Ory's Original Creole Jazz Band.

BIOGRAPHY:

King Oliver's Creole Jazz Band

Born in 1885 in Abend, Louisiana

King Oliver first learned to play the trombone, but he soon switched to the cornet. As a child he had been blinded in one eye and so he often played seated, in a chair leaning against the wall, with a Derby hat tilted over the damaged eye. It is said that King was the first cornetist to play with mutes, bottles and cups in the cornet's bell style of playing, associated with the gentler days of the old South.

From 1908 to 1917, Oliver worked parades, gigs and occasional tours with a number of brass bands including the Olympia, the Magnolia, the Onward, the Eagle, and Allen's. He also worked as a sideman for Kid Ory's band when the Kid was at Pete Lala's. In March 1919, Oliver left for Chicago to join clarinettist Lawrence Duhe's band. He also worked in legendary bassist Bill Johnson's band. Oliver later took over Duhe's band up to 1921, and was able to gig at various Chicago nightclubs including the Deluxe Café, the Pekin Cabaret and Dreamland. In 1921, he travelled to the West Coast and led bands in the San Francisco Bay Area. In June 1922, Oliver returned to Chicago and organised his own Creole Jazz Band for a stay at the Lincoln Gardens. This was the band that achieved immortality in 1923 when they made their recording debut for the Gennett label. The Creole Jazz Band was revered by all the white musicians in Chicago who, when their own gigs were over,

would nightly make a pilgrimage to the Lincoln Gardens to hear Oliver's band which at that time had a very young Louis Armstrong playing second trumpet in his very first band outside of New Orleans. The band's Lincoln Gardens gigs lasted until December 1924, when Oliver formed the Dixie Syncopators for a stay at the Plantation Café. This group stayed together until 1927 and it was then that Oliver decided to try his luck in New York.

He was approached by several record companies to make records, but he turned down the offers fearing that other musicians would hear the songs and copy his style. Because of this, the first jazz group on record in New York was the Original Dixieland Jazz Band, and so they attracted all the early fame and glory, rather than Oliver.

Oliver died in 1938.

THE BRASS BANDS:

About the time of the American Civil War, most towns had a bandstand, or belvedere, set up in a park. There was no radio or records and so at weekends a small, 4- to 8-piece brass band would entertain the townspeople. Dressed in their uniforms, they must have made a very imposing sight. Probably, these bands, were the prototype for the bands of New Orleans and other towns, too.

When we think of old New Orleans, the mind conjures up an image of street parades with Papa Jack Laine's Brass Band leading the way, or bands riding through town with a horse-drawn wagon advertising a dance, or funeral processions with the band playing 'Nearer My God To Thee', 'When The Saints Go Marchin' In' or 'Didn't He Ramble?', as in the James Bond movie *Live and Let Die*.

White and black musicians listened avidly to each other's playing. The black musicians tried to learn from the better-educated, smoother-playing white bands, and the white bands tried to capture the essence of the rougher black music. Accordingly, there was a parallel musical development by both black and white bands Tom Anderson's Café was a major musical centre in Storyville at Basin and Iberville Streets. Just a few doors up was the Mahogany Hall, now best remembered for the jazz tune 'Mahogany Hall Stomp'.

As mentioned previously, there were many white bands in New Orleans of which Papa Jack Laine's was the best known. Members of his band, including his son Albert, went on to form their own bands. The most famous of these was Nick LaRocca, whose Original Dixieland Jazz Band achieved worldwide fame, as well as introducing jazz to New York and London. There was a huge number of white marching brass bands throughout the midwest and south, many of which marched by day, and played the bars and cabarets at night.

Another of the early big band innovators in New Orleans was Jelly Roll Morton.

Above: A street band marching through old New Orleans.

BIOGRAPHY:
Jelly Roll Morton

Born 20 September 1885 in New Orleans, Louisiana

In 1904 Morton began his musical career by playing piano in the halls of New Orleans brothels. He got his name when he saw a black vaudeville comedian announce himself as "Sweet Papa Cream Puff, right out of the bakery shop". In the street slang of old New Orleans, words such as cream puff, biscuit and jelly roll were common euphemisms for sexual organs and intercourse and so, never one to be upstaged, Morton began to introduce himself as "Papa Jelly Roll, with stove pipes in my hips and all the women in town dyin' to turn my damper down".

In the early 1900s earning a living was quite difficult for a black American musician and so Jelly Roll did other work to supplement his income including pimping, tailoring, pool-hustling, card-sharking, and bell-hopping as well as his piano-playing. In 1908 he left New Orleans and toured cities on the Gulf of Mexico coast and in Texas. He also went to St Louis and visited Scott Joplin. After a brief tour with a minstrel show, he went to live in California for five years from 1917.

In 1922 he had a fairly well established reputation as a musician, songwriter, bandleader of his Red Hot Peppers Orchestra and arranger. Later on in that year he moved his operations to Chicago which had become the centre of the jazz world. In 1927, he moved to New York where he also had great success. Then in 1929 the Depression hit and shortly thereafter Benny Goodman introduced the world to swing.

Dixieland or jazz music went into decline and Morton suffered during those hard years, even having to pawn the diamond in his front tooth. Some of Jelly's compositions were still being played, but he received little or no royalties, and he fell into obscurity. In California, his health began to fail and he died in Los Angeles on 10 July 1941.

In 1913, another first happened when James Reese Europe's Society Orchestra became the first African-American band to record. He made recordings for the Victor Talking Machine Company and a series of recordings for the Pathé Talking Machine and Record Company in 1919. He also put together the first big band – and it was big!

Above: Jelly Roll Morton.

BIOGRAPHY:

James Reese Europe

Born 22 February 1880 in Mobile, Alabama

In 1890, James Reese Europe and his family moved to Washington DC and it was there that he received his music education in the city's public schools, studying both piano and violin. In 1905, he settled in New York, where he worked as a pianist in the local clubs and worked on some musical comedies. He also met and performed with Bob Cole, the Johnson Brothers and the Williams and Walker Company vaudeville teams.

In 1910, he organised some Harlem jazz musicians into a group called The Clef Club. This club soon turned into a combination of orchestra, booking agency and black musicians' union. In May 1912, they made musical history when they played a benefit for the Colored Music Settlement School at New York's famed Carnegie Hall. The 125-member Clef Club orchestra that he conducted that night featured some rather extraordinary instrumentation, including 47 mandolins, bandores and 27 harp-guitars. It was the very first time that a jazz band had played there. Previously, most Afro-American groups had been limited to banjo and bone-playing in minstrel shows, so this performance represented a very real breakthrough for the black musical community of the time.

During the 1910s, dancers Vernon and Irene Castle had become widely popular entertainers with their public dance exhibitions.

They asked Europe to accompany them on their American and European dance tours and, in 1914, Europe signed a contract to tour England, France and other countries, with the Castles. The Castles were extremely successful and they soon opened a dance school called The Castle House and also a supper club called Sans Souci. Europe's Society Orchestra provided the music for these rather successful ventures. Because of this activity, Europe's Society Orchestra was offered a recording contract with Victor records marking the first time that an Afro-American Orchestra was offered a contract with a major American record label. However, the outbreak of World War 1 changed those plans.

In 1917, the United States formally declared war on Germany. On 18 September 1916, Europe enlisted in the 15th New York Infantry, Harlem's black National Guard regiment. A week later, Noble Sissle, a friend and fellow musician also joined. Europe completed his officer training and was about to assume command of a machine-gun company, when Colonel William Haywood asked him to organise a band for the US. 15th Infantry, who were renamed the 369th Regiment of the US Army and sent to France. There they became the first African-American combat troops. Europe's band, nicknamed the Harlem Hellfighters, performed for the troops, for the French people and for government officials and so brought jazz to France.

Above: James Reese Europe.

Above: Owing to Bix Beiderbecke's influence (far right), soloists were given
"space" in each tune and the music was more forcefully presented to the audience.

On 17 February 1919, 1,300 black heroes returned from the war, every one of them decorated, with the Croix de Guerre by the French Government. Over a million people watched them parade up Fifth Avenue in lower Manhattan to Harlem. The Harlem Hellfighters band led the troops and, as they turned off 110th Street onto Lenox Avenue, the band broke out into the song 'Here Comes My Daddy Now'.

Sadly, a year later, Europe was killed by a crazed band-member. On 9 May, two days after their last recording session for Pathé, Europe reportedly reprimanded his drummer, Herbert Wright, because of Wright's habit of walking on and off stage while other acts were per-forming. At some point in the conversation, Wright took a pen knife from his pocket and stabbed Europe in the neck. Europe was rushed to hospital, but died soon afterwards.

During World War 1 a slow exodus of musicians had begun to move up-river to Chicago. Other musicians went west to Kansas City and to California, while many others drifted up to St Louis and Detroit.

Chicago was a good location for several reasons: it was easy to get to and it was straight up the river;. there was a growing black population; and there were good employment prospects in the stockyards and outlying steel mill jobs. With Prohibition in force, Chicago also became a magnet for bootleggers and thus the centre of a flourishing night life. In the smaller clubs, playing for black audiences, there were small 3- or 4- man groups playing, usually with a kazoo or washboard, much the same kind of music they had played back home in New Orleans.

In Chicago the music began to reflect the life there; it was a hard-driving, hustling and bustling city of stock-yards, businesses, saloons, gangsters, bootleg "hooch" and jazz. Owing to Bix Beiderbecke's influence, soloists were given "space" in each tune and the music was more forcefully presented to the audience.

The 1920s are still described as "the Jazz Age". Ladies bobbed their hair and wore shorter-length dresses and skirts and lipstick. Men dressed in the new styles of suits and slicked down their hair. It seemed that the entire world was listening to and dancing to jazz. As a variety of musicians began moving into Chicago, the music started to change. In the larger clubs and vaude-ville theatres, a smoother musical style developed, with larger bands and increasing use of arrangements.

Today, all that remains of original New Orleans jazz are the recordings of the Chicago bands. This is because there was no recording company in New Orleans. Jazz was changing. In New Orleans, the music was played in ensemble style but in Chicago a method of playing developed that emphasised the solos of the band members. This period saw the debut of such solo vir-tuosi as Bix Beiderbecke, Benny Goodman; Gene Krupa and, of course, "Satchmo".

LET'S DANCE

CHICAGO

In 1921, the first white orchestra from New Orleans to play in Chicago was led by the trombonist, Tom Brown. In 1922, Stein's Dixie Jass Band followed (with Nick LaRocca on cornet).

Before that, in 1920, Paul Mares and George Brunies (trombone) were working a Mississippi riverboat that stopped at Davenport, Iowa. There they teamed up with Leon Rapolo (cornet), a white New Orleans musician, and a young local cornetist named Bix Beiderbecke. In time, they added Elmer Schobel (piano), Frank Snyder (drums), Louis Black (banjo) and Alfred Loyacano (bass). They were hired by the Friar's Club in Chicago, first calling themselves the Friar's Society Orchestra, but later changing their name to the New Orleans Rhythm Kings.

Above: Bix Beiderbecke (1927).

BIOGRAPHY:

Bix Beiderbecke

Born 10 March 1903 in Davenport, Iowa

Beiderbecke came from a long line of musicians. As a child he studied music and learned to sight-read, something he was never fully proficient at, but he was able to play complex pieces from an early age. In addition to his excellent jazz phrasing, he is remembered today for a wonderfully clear bell-like tone that he could elicit from the cornet. Ironically, he was never formally trained in the cornet and played it left-handed for the first eight years.

Above: The young Bix Beiderbecke.

"Jazz came to America three hundred years ago in chains."

PAUL WHITEMAN

In 1921, while at Lake Forest Academy, he formed the Cy-Bix Orchestra with Walter "Cy" Welge (drums). He was expelled from school in 1922, mainly due to his interest in alcohol taking precedence over his interest in studying. In his short career, he played with some very popular performers of the day, including Hoagy Carmichael, Frankie Trumbauer, the Wolverines, Jean Goldkette and the Paul Whiteman Orchestra. He was briefly the leader of a group called Bix Beiderbecke and his Gang. The Whiteman and Goldkette bands used intricate arrangements that made real demands on a sight-reader. Fortunately his musical "ear" saved him. His friend Hoagy has written that Bix's ear was so precise that "he could identify the pitch of a belch".

In 1923, Bix joined the Wolverines, in 1924 he joined and left Jean Goldkette's band, then joined Frankie Trumbauer and played with Jean Goldkette's band again until it dispersed in 1928. During the period of February 1927 to May 1927, Bix and Frankie Trumbauer were to make a series of recordings for Okeh Records which are viewed as the peak of Beiderbecke's career.

Sadly, his alcohol problem was to plague his short but brilliant career. In January 1929, while playing with the Paul Whiteman Orchestra he was forced to leave the band suffering with delirium tremens. He was admitted to a Cleveland hospital where he had to have 24-hour

nursing. In February 1929 he left the hospital to rejoin the band in New York. There, he was badly beaten up by unknown assailants and was forced to return home to Davenport, Iowa, to recuperate.

In March 1929 he rejoined the band but in September, during a New York studio recording session, Beiderbecke suffered a major relapse. He returned to Davenport, Iowa, while Paul Whiteman kept him on full pay. In January 1930 Bix briefly played with the Jimmy Hicks Orchestra in Davenport and in February went

to Chicago to sit in with Wingy Manone's band and the Ted Weems' band.

In April 1930 Bix left for New York City, but did not feel he was ready to rejoin Whiteman's orchestra. Instead, he began playing some minor one-night shows before re-joining Whiteman. One October night he passed out in the middle of his solo and again returned to Davenport to recuperate, going on to New York to play with the Casa Loma Orchestra, although he only stayed with them for four days. His mental state was

such that he could not cope with their exacting routines. Bad depression combined with heavy drinking caused Beiderbecke to drift aimlessly around New York City rooming with various friends and in various apartments. While staying in the apartment of bass player George Kraslow, he took to playing cornet solos in the middle of the night.

Sadly, on 6 August 1931, after only 10 years as a jazz cornetist, Bix Beiderbecke died, due to complications related to his alcoholism.

Above: The Paul Whiteman Orchestra.

Nick LaRocca and the Original Dixieland Jazz Band had created a huge demand for the new "jazz" music. The Original Dixieland Jazz Band went to New York City, where they became the defining group for the city's style, and then on to London. Through this the New Orleans Rhythm Kings became the mainstay of Chicago jazz. They first recorded in 1922, after some personnel changes that strengthened the band. Oddly, by 1925, the group had folded leaving just a few recordings but a lasting impression on all future jazz artists, particularly with their Chicago jazz style. Their playing truly inspired Chicagoans, especially a small group of Austin High School students that originally included Jimmy and Richard McPartland, Frankie Teschemacher, Bud Freeman and Jim Lanigan on piano. This group of students listened to the the New Orleans Rhythm Kings' recordings, literally teaching themselves to play music by emulating what they heard on the records. They first called themselves the Austin High Gang, but later changed their name to the Austin Blue Friars. They were then joined by Dave North on piano with Lanigan moving to bass and Dave Tough, from the Lewis Institute in Oak Park, Illinois was introduced on drums. Still later, Floyd O'Brien came in on trombone.

Other Chicagoans that must be mentioned are Eddie Condon (banjo and guitar), Joe Sullivan and Art Hodes (both piano), Muggsy Spanier (cornet), Mezz Mezzrow (clarinet), and, of course, Benny Goodman and Gene Krupa.

Side Note:
In theme – the first piece the band plays
Out theme – the last piece the band plays

BIOGRAPHY:

Benny Goodman -The King of Swing

Born 30 May 1909, Chicago
In-theme: 'Let's Dance'
Out-theme: 'Goodbye'

As a child, Goodman studied music at the Hull House in Chicago. He was an integral part of the early group of musicians in Chicago, nowadays collectively known as The Chicagoans, that included Pee Wee Russell, Frankie Teschemacher, Leon Rapolo, Max Kaminsky, Jimmy McPartland and his brother Richard, Muggsy Spanier, the Dorsey brothers, Glenn Miller, and many others. As such, Benny can be considered one of the inventors of the modern American swing band.

In 1922, he appeared onstage with the Benny Meroff Orchestra, in Chicago, doing an imitation of Ted Lewis the clarinettist, who was then America's favourite. Not long afterwards, Ben Pollack sent for him to join the Pollack Orchestra. at the Venice ballroom in LA. Goodman's first recorded solo, 'He's the Last Word', was with the Pollack Orchestra, in Chicago on 12 December 1926. He left Pollack in 1929 and became a successful studio musician in New York City. In the summer of 1932 Goodman formed his first band, starring singer Russ Columbo.

In the aftermath of the Depression of 1929 to 1933, a new generation of young people were looking for music that they could call their own. Goodman's orchestra was destined to fill this need. The hot bands of the 1920s and early 1930s like Fletcher Henderson's, Coon-Sanders' Nighthawks, and Don Redman's had all been disbanded. The only real competition Goodman had was the Casa-Loma Orchestra.

In 1934 he formed his second band, which had more regular work with a residency at Billy Rose's Music Hall. Along with making some interesting recordings, the band appeared on the three-hour coast-to-coast NBC radio programme called *Let's Dance*. Goodman's orchestra shared the *Let's Dance* radio show with the Kel Murray Orchestra, a straight-ahead dance band, and Xavier Cugat's Latin Waldorf-Astoria Hotel Orchestra, a society dance band.

NBC's *Let's Dance* radio show was actually a five-hour broadcast from New York staged so that all US .time zones would get three hours of music. The east coast and central time zones were cut off after the first three hours; mountain time zone listened to hours 2–4, while the West Coast listened to hours 3–5. In this manner, American listeners heard three solid hours of dance music over the airwaves. Six months later, MCA booked Benny's orchestra for a coast- to-coast tour which turned out to be almost totally unsuccessful and on several occasions during the tour MCA considered cancelling. That was until the band reached its last date at the Palomar Ballroom in Los Angeles. There Goodman finally found his audience. The kids went completely wild over Goodman's big band swing sound which soon swept the country. When he brought his orchestra back to New York's Paramount theatre, the kids were actually dancing in the aisles. Bobbysox-ers were invented and jitterbugs became endemic. Benny Goodman was crowned as the King of Swing, a title he was to hold for the rest of his life.

After his extended Palomar engagement, the band headed back east, stopping over in Chicago for still another extended run, this time at the Joseph Urban Room at the Congress Hotel.

In 1935, Benny Goodman and his orchestra played the Congress Hotel in Chicago. The band included such outstanding musicians as Gene Krupa on drums; Jess Stacy, piano; Nate Kabier, trumpet; Hymie Shertzer, alto sax; Art Rollini, tenor sax; Allen Reuss, guitar; Harry Goodman (Benny's brother), bass; and Helen Ward, one of the best big-band vocalists. Earlier, Goodman had made some trio recordings using Krupa and pianist Teddy Wilson that had sold well. Helen Oakley, later of Helen Oakley Dance, encouraged him to feature Wilson, who was black, in the trio at the hotel. Thankfully, Goodman was persuaded that featuring such a racially mixed group was not a recipe for disaster in those segregated times and the occasion passed without public comment. Wilson was soon to become a regular member of the Goodman trio. This was a turning point in American musical history. It was the first time that a white band hired a black musician to play with it on stage and Goodman continued with this system.

Above: Benny Goodman.

In 1936, Benny added Lionel Hampton, the vibraphonist, to form the Benny Goodman Quartet. Though this was not the first integrated jazz group, it had the highest profile by far. Goodman's big band was continuing to attract huge and enthusiastic audiences, and was featuring such sidemen as Harry James, Ziggy Elman, Chris Griffin, Vernon Brown, Babe Russin and Arthur Rollini. Starting in March 1937, Goodman began a particularly successful date at New York's Paramount theatre. His records were also selling well.

At the start, when Benny's orchestra was little known, it was basically a dance band, occasionally playing some "hot" music. There was little income and Benny was working hard to build up his band's "book". Before the 1934–1935 period, throughout it and afterward,s too, most of the Goodman orchestra's book had been written by Spud Murphy. The "Killer-Dillers" (like 'Sing, Sing, Sing') in the Goodman book were almost all written by Jimmy Mundy and Spud Murphy. Benny was also just beginning to pick up some scores from Fletcher Henderson.

In 1939, after Fletcher Henderson's Orchestra disbanded, Benny hired him. By this time, Goodman's orchestra was enormously successful. Fletcher then presented Benny with many of his own band's scores. Benny continued to use the scores of Fletcher and Horace Henderson, Edgar Sampson, Benny Carter and Deane Kincaide throughout his career. (Mary Lou Williams contributed the famous 'Roll 'Em'.) To Benny's credit, he never failed to give full credit to Fletcher for co-authorship of the big band swing sound (even though Benny himself played a huge part in the invention of that sound).

After Henderson, Benny went on to hire musicians such as Cootie Williams (trumpet), Charlie Christian (guitar) and "Slam" Stewart (bass fiddle) as well as singers such as Ella Fitzgerald and Jimmy Rushing, again all black artists.

Benny should also be remembered for establishing the "personality" concept in big band swing. It was with Benny's band that the sidemen were given public exposure as soloists. It was this fan worship for Goodman's sidemen such as Harry James, Gene Krupa, Lionel Hampton and Ziggy Elman that later allowed them to form their own orchestras. Among his female vocalists were Helen Ward, Peggy Lee and Louise Tobin. This practice of featuring the sidemen was picked up by virtually every other swing orchestra of the day. Rarely does Benny receive sufficient credit for this.

In 1939, Benny switched recording companies from RCA to Columbia. He also signed Eddie Sauter as his new arranger. It was Sauter who rejected Goodman's original brasses against the saxes format for a newer and more harmonically advanced type of scoring, especially for the ballads. Sauter was responsible for such hits as 'Clarinet à la King' and 'Benny Rides Again'. In 1941, Benny married Alice Duckworth, the sister of John Hammond, the famous jazz critic and another believer in racial equality. It was a very happy, long-lived marriage.

"Music washes away from the soul the dust of everyday life."

Red Auerbach

Another unique contribution of Benny's was the concept of a band within a band, with his magnificent trios (1935, quartet and sextet. The small group sessions with Hampton, Wilson and Krupa are as live and vibrant today as when they were first recorded – truly the hallmark of genius. After the end of the big band era, Goodman went on to a career as a classical clarinet soloist with many of the world's great symphony orchestras.

Nobody, but absolutely nobody, played the clarinet as well as Benny. He drilled his band to perfection by demanding no less from the sidemen than he did from himself. He was not only well liked by the bandsmen, but also very much admired for his musicianship. He stands as a giant among American jazz musicians.

He died on 13 June 1986 in New York.

Above: Benny Goodman.

Above: Gene Krupa – "the greatest drummer in the world".

BIOGRAPHY:

Gene Krupa

Born 15 January 1909, in Chicago
Theme songs:
First: 'Drum Boogie'
Early on c.1938: 'Apurksody' (Krupa spelled backward plus
the last syllable of "rhapsody")
Later on: 'Starburst'

Gene Krupa came out of Chicago in the 1920s, along with Benny Goodman, Eddie Condon, Red McKenzie and others. His mother had failed to get him into studying for the priesthood and so the rest of his family encouraged him to study music, which he did on a formal basis with several teachers, mainly Roy C. Knapp. His early influences came from listening to New Orleans jazz drummers such as Tubby Hall, Baby Dodds and Zutty Singleton. While still a teenager, he began playing in dance bands, including the Benson Orchestra, and with Al Gale and Joe Kayser amongst others.

In 1927 Gene made his very first record with a band formed by Eddie Condon, but fronted by Red McKenzie. Historically it is a landmark as Gene is reputed to be the first drummer to use both a bass drum and tom-toms. In 1929, the two Chicagoans, Eddie Condon and Gene Krupa, moved to New York City. The tough years of the Depression saw Krupa often playing in theatre pit bands led by Red Nichols, alongside such other sidemen as Glenn Miller and Benny Goodman. In the early 1930s he worked in the bands of Mal Hallett, Buddy Rogers, and with the singer Russ Columbo.

> *"A jazz musician is a juggler who uses harmonies instead of oranges."*
>
> BENNY GREEN

In 1934, he joined Benny Goodman's new orchestra. He was a key figure in forming the band's distinctive sound and was often found enthusiastically encouraging the other sidemen to do their best work. When the Goodman orchestra became a huge success in August 1935, Krupa's fame was to follow. There was a certain empathy between Krupa and Goodman. Benny brought out the very best in Gene, and Gene's rhythm work lifted the Goodman orchestra to a higher level. Later in his career, Krupa often spoke of his delight in playing with Benny Goodman.

Krupa is remembered as the man who, during the swing era, made the drum a popular "solo" instrument. His work on 'Sing, Sing, Sing' may be the best example of this. Also, from around 1937, it was Gene Krupa and Dave Tough who played dominant roles in establishing what is now the standard drum kit of bass drum, snare drum, tom-tom, floor tom, hi-hat and two to four suspended cymbals.

Great showmanship combined with his really good feeling for jazz "timing" made Krupa a truly desirable sideman. His style was actually relatively simplistic when compared to other drummers of the day.

It consisted mainly of a steady, heavy bass drum on every beat, a driving 2/4 high-hat rhythm and accented, syncopated tom-toms. However, his frequent alteration of the rhythm that had been set by the leader did not endear him to Goodman. Not long after the famous 1938 Carnegie Hall concert, Krupa and Goodman had a public quarrel, and Krupa left. It was then that he first formed his own big band.

This 1938 band, with Irene Daye and Leo Watson on vocals, consisted of Bob Snyder, Sam Donohue, Mascagni Ruffo, Sam Musiker all on saxophones; Nick Prospero, C. Frankhauser, Tom Goslin all on trumpets; Toby Tyler, Bruce Squires, Dalton Rizzotto all on trombones; Ray Biondo on guitar; Horace Rollins on bass; Milton Raskin on piano and Krupa naturally on the drums. In 1941, trumpeter Roy Eldridge and vocalist Anita O'Day joined and the band's popularity soared. The success proved short-lived, however, because Krupa was jailed in the aftermath of a San Francisco drug-bust. He was found guilty and received a 1–6 year sentence, but was released on bail pending an appeal.

He returned to New York and rejoined the Goodman orchestra, then touring US Army bases on the east coast. Krupa opted to stay behind when Goodman took the band on an extended national tour, fearing the public would react badly toward him and so, by association, to Goodman's band. He joined the Tommy Dorsey Orchestra for an engagement at New York's Paramount theatre. Krupa

received a tumultuous welcome when he came on stage, and this proved to be an emotional milestone in his rehabilitation. Then his jail sentence was overturned on appeal, as a judge ruled that the charges against him had been filed improperly. Krupa left Dorsey and formed a new band.

The band had a somewhat shaky start. Gene did not quite know just where his position in the band should be. Sometimes, he would front it and wave a baton, while at other times he was on the drummer's throne. His early relations with the band were also a little disturbed as he saw himself as the star, rather than just the leader. Eventually, though, the band did begin to straighten out. During the break at a one-night ballroom show, the owner approached him and told him that it was not necessary for every single tune to have a drum solo, which was an unsettling moment for Krupa. Krupa kept his band going throughout the 1940s, and even adapted somewhat to "bop" style when he used scores by Gerry Mulligan, and sidemen such as Don Fagerquist, Charlie Ventura and Red Rodney. However, the big band era had ended and in 1951 Krupa disbanded. After that, he kept busy playing with a small group (usually a quartet), did some light touring, and even opened a drum school with fellow drummer William "Cozy" Cole.

The 1960s often found him at reunions of the Goodman Quartet, along with Lionel Hampton and Teddy Wilson, but his health started to fail due to heart trouble.

He did recover from this but was later diagnosed with leukaemia. In the 1970s, he limited his work to New York City, and his performances with the Goodman Quartet were almost always preceded by a blood transfusion. Krupa died of leukaemia, on 16 October 1973 in Yonkers, New York.

Although the Chicagoans, were representative of "new" Dixielanders. Most were not from New

Orleans, but had absorbed the music. And, along the way, they improved it greatly. On the north side of Chicago were the white musicians, such as Muggsy Spanier, Bunny Berigan, "Wingy" Manone (one-armed cornetist from New Orleans), George Wettling and Eddie Condon. On the south side of Chicago, were the black musicians such as Jimmy Noone, Lovie Austin, Johnny Dodds, Joe "King" Oliver and the legendary Louis Armstrong.

Above: The Goodman Quartet.

Above: Louis Armstrong.

BIOGRAPHY:

Louis Armstrong

Born 4 August 1901, in New Orleans, Louisiana
Theme songs:
Early: 'On the Sunny Side of the Street'
Later: 'When It's Sleepy Time Down South'

Louis Armstrong, born Daniel Louis Armstrong, was deserted by his father at the age of 11 and left with a mother who was only rarely around. He grew up on some of the most desolate, squalid streets of the New Orleans "red light" area and was forced into singing on the streets for whatever little change that passers-by would offer.

At the age of 13 Louis was arrested for celebrating New Year's Eve by shooting a gun in the street. He was sent to the Colored Waifs Home For Boys. There he studied the cornet and played in the Waifs' Home band, which was then under the direction of Paul Davis. Louis, nicknamed "Satchmo" (derived from "Satchelmouth"), would later say "Me and music got married at the home."

In the following years Armstrong played with virtually all of New Orleans' best black bands including Fate Marable's riverboat band and the Kid Ory Orchestra. Not long after leaving the orphanage, he wrote the song 'I Wish I Could Shimmy Like My Sister Kate', which is still a jazz standard. The tune is formally credited to another great Dixieland leader, Armand Piron, but Armstrong always claimed he wrote the song and sold it to Piron for a few dollars, although during his career Armstrong never played the tune. In 1922, Joe King Oliver and his Creole Jazz Band were in Chicago and he offered Louis a job that he stayed in for about a year. Louis often told historians that King Oliver was his real mentor. In 1923 Louis recorded for the first time with King Oliver. After his stay with Oliver, Louis took over trumpet duty with the Fletcher Henderson Orchestra, one of the great early big bands. During these years, Armstrong also recorded with Oliver, Henderson and Clarence Williams, and even with blues singer, Bessie Smith.

In 1925 through to 1928, Armstrong made an important group of recordings with his Hot Five and Hot Seven groups. During this period he re-invented jazz. He established the soon-to-be standard 4/4 swing tempo and the theme-solo-theme structure. He further defined the concept of jazz itself, which he had absorbed while listening to Bix Beiderbecke, with the soloist at the very centre, no longer playing short, simple "breaks" with slight melodic embellishment, but playing fully improvised, chord-based solos of a whole chorus or longer. He described a progression from the melody, to routining the melody, to routining the routine. Through this basic model of jazz performance, Armstrong created the vocabulary that virtually all future jazz soloists would use.

THE KING is COMING

Byron "Speed" Reilly
Takes Pleasure in Presenting—

THE GREATEST OF
★ ATTRACTIONS ★

LOUIE ARMSTRONG

WITH HIS ORIGINAL
FAMOUS ORCHESTRA

MON. DEC. 20
Sweet's Ballroom
Franklin at 14th St., Oakland, Calif.

ADM. $1.00   DANCE 'till 2

DOORS OPEN — 8:30 p.m.

In Person

The Trumpet
The Personality
The King Himself
With Songs and Hot Tunes
Louie Armstrong

DOORS OPEN —

Oh Boy!—Wh
An A Galaxy

★ Maestro LUI
AT THE F

★ Miss Bobbie (
HOW THIS BA

★ Henry "Red"
"SATCHMO'S"

★ Sonny Wood
YOU'LL LIKE

18   ARTISTS
SEE and HEAR

Louie
"KING of th

SWI
Monday

---

*"Be good if I get to the
Pearly Gates ...
I'll play with Gabriel."*

LOUIS ARMSTRONG

Armstrong also had a knack for borrowing other people's orchestras whereby the orchestra's role was to showcase Satchmo at his best. In 1928, he, "borrowed" Carroll Dickerson's (fiddler) Band. Next he borrowed the Cocoanut Grove Orchestra, later known as the Blue Rhythm Band. In 1930, he borrowed Les Hite's Orchestra (with Lionel Hampton, Marshall Royal and Lawrence Brown), and re-named it Louis Armstrong's Sebastian New Cotton Club Orchestra. From 1929 to 1941, Louis fronted the great Luis Russell

Orchestra. On occasion, during this period, he would record with the Dorsey Brothers, the Casa Loma Orchestra or Andy Iona and his Islanders.

Louis fronted large bands (rarely less than 15 musicians) during most of the 1930s through to the early 1950s. His fame was worldwide and he developed a reputation for being a friendly, warm personality which stayed with him throughout his life.

In 1965 he was asked to record a few songs in New York before leaving for an extended tour overseas. Months later while in London the band was asked many times to play 'Dolly'. Finally Louis asked his manager what these people were requesting. It was at that time that Louis was told that one of the songs he had recorded in New York was a huge hit in the States. The song, 'Hello Dolly', was such a huge hit that it even knocked the Beatles out of the top spot for the first time.

In 1928 a German "avant-garde" opera appeared called *The Three Penny Opera*, by Kurt Weill (music) and Bertold Brecht (lyrics and libretto) and was somewhat obscure even to the most avid of opera fans. One day, Louis recorded a song from the opera, in his own inimitable Dixieland style, called 'Mac The Knife' ('Mackie Die Messer' in German). It was an instantaneous worldwide hit. His rendition made the opera well known even to non-opera fans around the world. Lotte Lenya, who was the composer's wife, telephoned Louis to thank him for his wonderful version.

"Not too slow, not too fast. Kind of half-fast!"

LOUIS ARMSTRONG

The US State Department sent his orchestra on official tours to countries around the world and he was referred to as "America's Musical Ambassador". Armstrong's legacy to American music, and indeed the world's music, is outstanding as was his rise from such humble and impoverished beginnings. He influenced virtually every musician who came after him and his phraseology is so deeply embedded in American popular song that today virtually no one can tell they are thinking, singing and playing in a style developed by Louis Armstrong.

Louis Armstrong died on 6 July 1971 in New York.

The Great Depression, which began in 1929 and lasted through the 1930s, altered the lives of musicians drastically. It destroyed the mid-western independent recording companies, such as Gennett. The end of Prohibition certainly altered Chicago's nightlife. Most of the "Chicagoans" now moved to New York City. New York was the home of the leading radio networks and recording companies as well as a stellar array of hotel "rooms", supper clubs and the famous 52nd Street, which was referred to by some as "Swing Street". Chicago style was ending and New York jazz was starting.

TAKE THE "A" TRAI

NEW YORK – TIN PAN ALLEY

In the early 1910s, the music publishers were located in and around Union Square, in New York City, near the theatres. By the early 1920s, the publishing companies had moved to West 28th Street, between Broadway and Sixth Avenue. One of the newspapers sent their reporter Rosenfield (who was to become a composer in his own right) down to the publishing district to get background on a story he was to write. He wrote that the babble and noise coming from the open windows of the music publishing offices sounded like "so many tin pans being beaten". From then on the term "Tin Pan Alley" became synonymous with the song-publishing business. The publishers would place newspaper strips between the strings of the piano to muffle the sound which did nothing to improve the tone. By the late 1920s, the publishers had begun a slow migration to the area from 42nd Street to 50th Street. Finally, most of the publishers settled into the Brill Building on 50th Street and Broadway and are still there to this day.

An array of piano merchants supplied pianos to the composers and publishers in Tin Pan Alley. The most famous of these was a shop called Tonk Pianos and the owner Mr Tonk tried to make sure it was his piano sounds coming out of every open window. Thus yet another legendary musical term was born as visitors to Tin Pan Alley said it was filled with "honky tonk" sounds. Indeed a great many blues songs came out of Tin Pan Alley.

"Jazz will endure just as long as people hear it through their feet instead of their brains."

JOHN PHILIP SOUSA

Above: The Brill Building on 50th Street and Broadway in New York.

HARLEM IN PROHIBITION TIMES

Harlem was "segregated" right up to about the early 1920s when it was an all-white, predominantly Irish neighbourhood. Later on, the Irish migrated to the upper tip of Manhattan.

Clustered between 125th Street and 135th Street and between Lenox and Seventh Avenues in Harlem, over 125 entertainment places were active during the 1920s and 1930s. There were speakeasies, taverns, cellars, lounges, cafés, supper clubs, rib joints, theatres, dance halls and an ever-changing number of bars and grills.

There were 10 theatres around the neighbourhood, all of which were segregated apart from the Alhambra, located on Seventh Avenue, and the Crescent, which were black only. The great blues singer Bessie Smith played the Alhambra in 1927. The other theatres included the Douglas, the Harlem Opera House (dating back to 1889, it was the oldest), the Lafayette (Seventh Avenue), the Odeon, the Oriental and the Lincoln (135th Street). It was at the Lincoln theatre, owned by Milton Gusdorfer, that in the 1920s Fats Waller played the organ to accompany the silent motion pictures. In 1922 Frank Schiffman and Leo Brecher purchased the Harlem Opera House. A very young Ella Fitzgerald was discovered there during an amateur night contest by Bardu Ali, a sideman in Chick Webb's orchestra.

The most famous theatre in Harlem was the Apollo, originally known as The Hurtig and Seamon's Burlesque but renamed as the Apollo on 26 January 1934. It was located on 125th Street and had a 1,750 capacity. Many black artists launched their career at the amateur nights held at the world-renowned theatre. Performances ran seven days a week at 12:30, 3:30, 6:30 and 9:30 pm, with an additional midnight show on Wednesday, Saturday and Sunday. The contracts were for performing 31 shows over a one-week period.

Harlem was in its swinging heyday from the mid-1920s to the mid-1930s. There were a lot of ballrooms there as well as theatres, and visitors from all over the world, as well as the local New Yorkers, came to Harlem for an evening of pleasure and the latest "hot" entertainment. On 142nd and Lenox Avenue there was the Douglas theatre which also contained the infamous Cotton Club on the second floor; on 132nd Street was the Congress Casino; and on West 135th Street was the Golden Gate. The entire block from 141st to 142nd Street was the world-famous Savoy Ballroom, between 138th and 139th Streets was the Garden of Joy, a dance hall enclosed in canvas, and then at the corner of 125th Street and Seventh Avenue was the still-famous Rose Danceland.

In New York, it is said, all the clubs were run by gangsters. The "big four" clubs were the Cotton Club, Connie's Inn, Smalls Paradise and Barron Wilken's Club – although there were several hundred more.

Above: Harlem's legendary Apollo theatre.

Above: Louis Armstrong at the Cotton Club.

THE COTTON CLUB

The Cotton Club started life as Club Deluxe which belonged to fighter Jack Johnson. It was failing as a business and so the infamous gangster Owney Madden, with the blessing and financial backing of Al Capone, took it over. Madden was a leading bootlegger and needed the club as an outlet during Prohibition for his illegal "hooch". In 1923, after a redecoration and renaming, the Cotton Club opened its doors.

Madden operated a "whites only" policy – the club's manager, George "Big Frenchy" Demange, even turned away W.C. Handy, the publisher. Madden's thugs also kept out inter-racial couples. The Cotton Club was nicknamed "the Aristocrat of Harlem" as guests like the Mayor of New York, movie stars like George Raft and the society hostess Emily Vanderbilt went there. The revues were all written by whites such as Harold Arlen, Ted Koehler, Jimmy McHugh and Dorothy Fields, and produced by Lew Leslie. The high-calibre black talent ensured the club was a huge success, though.

On the club's first night it was Fletcher Henderson's band that opened. A young Coleman Hawkins and an equally young Don Redman were in the band.

Fletcher "Smack" Henderson

Born 18 December 1897 in Cuthbert, Georgia
Theme song: 'Christopher Columbus'

Henderson first learned to play piano at the age of six. His brother, Horace also became a bandleader and arranger. By the time Henderson was in high school, he was an accomplished pianist. He graduated from Atlanta University and moved to New York City to attend graduate school at Columbia University in order to pursue a career in chemistry. In New York, he was hired as a song plugger by the W.C. Handy music publishing company. In 1920 Handy's partner, Harry Pace, left to form the Black Swan Phonograph Company. Henderson became the new record company's musical director but only until 1924 when it was absorbed by J. Mayo Williams, a Paramount Records recording director. In 1927, Williams founded another shortlived black recording enterprise called Black Patti. Although there was a market for black recording companies, limited finances meant they frequently went under. Fortunately Vocalion Records hired Williams as a talent scout.

In 1922, Fletcher's band opened at the Club Alabam. The sidemen consisted of Charlie "Big" Green on trombone, Howard Scott and Elmer Chambers on trumpets, and Don Redman and Coleman Hawkins on saxophones. The rhythm section had Bob Escudero on tuba, Charlie Dixon on banjo, Kaiser Marshall on drums and Henderson on piano. The rhythm section stayed the same for many years, while Coleman Hawkins stayed with Fletcher for a decade.

On 12 March 1926, Henderson was the first act on at New York's Savoy Ballroom's opening night. Additions to the line-up on that night were Buster Bailey (clarinet) and Louis "Satchmo" Armstrong.

In 1927 the band line-up was Jimmy Harrison and Benny Morton on trombone; June Cole was on tuba; Marshall on drums; Dixon on banjo; Don Pasquall, Buster Bailey and Coleman Hawkins on saxophones; and Tommy Ladnier, Joe Smith and Russell Smith were the trumpeters. 1931 saw yet another Fletcher Henderson Orchestra line-up with sidemen John Kirby on bass; Coleman Hawkins, Russell Procope and Edgar Sampson on saxophones; Rex Stewart, Bobby Stark and Russell Smith on trumpets; J.C. Higginbotham and Sandy Williams on trombones; Clarence Holiday on guitar; Walter Johnson on drums and Henderson still on the piano.

Although some historians cite Henderson as the inventor of swing, over and above Benny Goodman, it is rather Henderson's invention of "block passages" that is undisputed. Block passages are where a section, say the brass, play the same line together. Later, this came to be a standard with the big swing bands. When Henderson's own orchestra was disbanded he joined Benny Goodman, contributing many of the scores that Henderson's own band had been playing in the 1920s. This meant that the "block passages" technique was also apparent in Benny's scores.

Still other historians note that, while Benny did in fact use many Henderson scores, he did not use them till later. Fletcher joining the Goodman band was a notable occasion; it was the first time that a white band had hired a black man to work on stage with the orchestra.

Henderson took the freewheeling New Orleans jazz sound of trumpet, trombone and clarinet front line and incorporated it into the big band by making each instrument the lead of a four-man section. Together with a four-man rhythm backing, this format was able to carry forward the drive and syncopation of the original New Orleans jazz bands, eventually culminating in the "swing" of Benny Goodman, and then others. In addition, many of the wonderfully talented young musicians who first worked with Henderson would go on to great careers with other swing bands.

The Cotton Club put on two revues per year for the next 16 years. Lew Leslie was the earliest producer of the club's revues, which featured six "Lovely Tan" chorines and six dancing chorus boys, comics and all manner of vaudevillians. The team of Dorothy Fields and Jimmy McHugh were greatly responsible for the great music heard in those early revues.

They were later followed by another wonderful songwriting team – Ted Koehler and Harold Arlen. Some of the fastest-stepping revues in New York were found here. Lena Horne started her career here as a 16-year-old chorine. In 1923, Duke Ellington had been booked into the Kentucky Club, where he remained for five years. In 1927, the leader of the Cotton Club's house unit died and Ellington moved on to the Cotton Club until 1931, during which time he composed 'East St Louis Toodle-oo' (with his trumpeter Bubber Miley), the band's theme song; 'Black and Tan Fantasy'; 'The Mooch'; and 'Creole Love Call', a hit vocal for the band's singer, Adelaide Hall.

Above: The young Duke.

Duke Ellington

Born 29 April 1899 in Washington, DC
Theme songs:
Early on: 'East St Louis Toodle-oo'
Later on: 'Take the "A" Train'

Edward Kennedy Ellington – nicknamed "Duke" for his wit and elegance – had his first small band in Washington. In 1923, Ellington moved to New York City where he got a job playing with the Elmer Snowden Orchestra at the Hollywood Inn, off Broadway in the Times Square district. When the bandsmen discovered that Snowden was dividing the money incorrectly, they ousted him and elected Ellington as the new bandleader. The Hollywood Inn was a small "joint", and owned by disreputable people. Somewhat airless, the club had to be closed down during the summertime due to the intense heat inside. Accordingly, the owners would often arrange to have a convenient "fire" during the summertime, when the club was closed. They would then use the insurance money to rebuild the club for a new opening. In 1925 or 1926, after just such a fire, the club was rebuilt and re-opened as the Washington Club, and the Ellington band was now called the Washingtonians.

By 1927, he had become involved with band agent Irving Mills, who signed Ellington to a contract that gave Mills 50 per cent of Ellington's earnings and 55 per cent of any song royalties from Ellington's compositions. It was Mills who arranged Ellington's booking at the Cotton Club. His music became known as "jungle style" with some of his recordings of the time credited as "Duke Ellington and the Jungle Band". His singers

were Adelaide Hall, Ivie Anderson, Ray Nance and Kay Davis. Adelaide Hall was one of the chorus girls in the old Cotton Club. One day while the Duke was rehearsing the band for 'Creole Love Call', he overheard Adelaide humming an obbligato to the melody. The Duke heard it and asked her to do it in front of the band and on the recording. It was to become one of his biggest hits.

Ellington's crack team came together in the 1920s as a band with a common interest – drinking. During prohibition, the bandleader later recalled, he and his team laid into everything: kerosene, fermented apple juice, bathtub gin. It seems strange that this rough group would later evolve into one of the definitive big bands of the 1930s and 1940s, after Ellington assumed a leadership role and subsequently discovered a knack for writing. The Duke's talents lay in scoring around his band's respective skills, and it was under his tutelage that many legendary players developed their craft. Notables include "growl" trumpeter Bubber Miley, baritone saxist Harry Carney, alto Johnny Hodges, clarinettist Barney Bigard and trombonists "Tricky" Sam Nanton and Juan Tizol, who was to compose some of Ellington's biggest hits. Many of Ellington's sidemen went on to front their own projects, but none were able to repeat the creative heights they had reached with the Duke.

Ellington maintained a progressive outlook throughout his career; many of his original bandmates continued to share his vision and stayed with him for more than three decades. Some of his best work was in collaboration with arranger Billy Strayhorn, whose adventurous chord voicings blended seamlessly with those of the Duke and created some of the most enduring work of this century.

The Duke went on to write a great group of swing classics, as well as some "serious" music such as 'Black and Tan Fantasy', 'Harlem Airshaft' and 'Sophisticated Lady'.

In 1931 The Duke Ellington Band was replaced at the Cotton Club by Cab Calloway, the King of Heigh-de-ho.

Above: Ellington maintained a progressive outlook throughout his career; many of his original bandmates continued to share his vision and stayed with him for more than three decades.

Cab Calloway

Born 25 December 1907 in Rochester, New York
Theme song: 'Minnie The Moocher' (aka: 'Minnie the
Moocha')

Calloway was raised in Baltimore. His family moved to Chicago in his teens and it was there that he studied at Crane College. In the early 1920s, he made his first stage appearance in the *Plantation Days* show at the Loop theatre. In 1928, Cab was working as the master of ceremonies at the Sunset Cafe on Chicago's South Side. During a rehearsal, he decided to do a number with a band called Marion Hardy's Alabamians. The band was so impressed that they took a vote and made Cab their leader.

In January 1929, Cab took the band to New York City for a gig, but when the Alabamians went back to Chicago, he stayed in New York and took over the leadership of another band – The Missourians. In the spring of 1929, he returned to Chicago and again acted as both the master of ceremonies and the vocalist with the Alabamians.

In the following two years, his fate was again intertwined with these two bands. First, late in 1929, Cab returned to New York to appear on stage with the Hot Chocolate Revue before again rejoining the Alabamians for an appearance at the Savoy. In 1930, he was again presented with the opportunity to lead the Missourians, and again he accepted, but this time taking them to the Cotton Club as Cab Calloway and his Orchestra. His most famous hit song, 'Minnie the Moocher' was first broadcast from there. One night during a broadcast, Calloway's mind went blank and he forgot the lyrics. He started doing "scat" singing, to which the audience responded, and so he began to get the band involved, too. Thus the call-and-response technique, as exemplified in his hit song 'Heigh-de-ho', was born.

"Modern music is as dangerous as narcotics."

PIETRO MASCAGNI

Above: Cab Calloway.

In 1932, he went to Hollywood and appeared in several films, including *The Singing Kid* starring Al Jolson, *The Big Broadcast of 1933* and *Stormy Weather* – the latter starring a young Lena Horne, who sang the title song.

In 1938, Cab's band consisted of the following sidemen: Shad Collins, Irving Randolph, Doc Cheatham and Lammar Wright all on trumpet; Claude Jones, Keg Johnson, De Priest Wheeler on trombones; Chauncey Haughton and Andrew Brown on clarinet and alto sax; Walter Thomas and Chu Berry on tenor sax; Bennie Payne on piano; Danny Barker on guitar; Milton Hinton on string bass and Leroy Maxie on drums.

In the peak years of the 1940s he employed musicians such as Ben Webster and Hilton Jefferson on sax; Dizzy Gillespie and Jonah Jones on trumpets; and Cozy Cole on drums. Cab's big band lasted until 1948, attesting to his popularity. From 1948 to 1952, he mostly fronted small combos, but in 1951 Cab took a big band on tour to Montevideo. From June 1952 to August 1954, he appeared in the role of Sportin' Life with the touring company of Gershwin's opera *Porgy and Bess* across America and Europe.

From 1954 on, he worked as a solo act, although on occasion he did front a big band assembled by Eddie Barefield. He appeared in the 1980s film *The Blues Brothers* and died in 1994.

CONNIE'S INN

Connie's Inn opened in November 1921 as The Shuffle Inn, in honour of *Shuffle Along*, a hit Broadway show at the time. The inn was located at 2221 Seventh Avenue, on the corner of 131st Street and 7th Avenue – that is, in the basement next to the Lafayette theatre. In 1923 it was acquired by new owners, Connie and George Immerman, who were originally from Germany and ran a delicatessen in Harlem where the legendary Fats Waller was a delivery man. In June 1923 they moved the entrance from the 131st Street side to Seventh Avenue.

The house band was led by songwriter Luckey Roberts. In 1929, Louis Armstrong came to play there with Carroll Dickerson's orchestra. The floor show was Razaf and Waller's *Hot Chocolates* which later opened on Broadway featuring songs like 'Ain't Misbehavin''.

When it first opened Connie's was a whites-only club but later they did open their doors to black musicians, albeit when the white patrons had gone home.

Above: Cab Calloway and band, performing on stage.

Above: jazz dancing in Harlem.

SMALL'S PARADISE

Between 1917 and 1925, Ed Small owned The Sugar Cane Club over at 2212 Fifth Avenue. This may have been the first Harlem joint to attract the "swells" from downtown. In October 1925, Small opened The Paradise at 2294–1/2 Seventh Avenue. The club offered big band sessions and exotic floor shows with Creole chorus girls and dancing waiters that did the Charleston while bussing trays of food and illicit drinks. Piano-playing Charlie Johnson's orchestra was the house band for near 10 years. In 1932, they built a new police station nearby which somewhat deterred the bootleggers.

BARRON WILKEN'S 134TH ST AND 7TH AVE

Barron Wilken's Exclusive Club was located two blocks up from Connie's at 134 Street and 7th Avenue. It was a members-only club that opened at 11 pm but only really got going in the small hours of the morning.

Back in 1923, Duke Ellington had labelled the club the top spot in Harlem and the venue was known as "the rich man's black and white club". A US$100 bill did not stretch very far there, even during the Depression (the average weekly pay in the early 1930s was $16.00). Wilken catered for big spenders, gamblers, sports and women.

In 1926, Barron Wilken, "the night life king", was murdered by a drug addict/gambler named Yellow Charleston.

After the big four, there were many other lesser clubs; maybe 500 or more speakeasies were open in Harlem during prohibition and they stayed open all night.

THE SAVOY BALLROOM AND THE LINDY HOP

In the 1920s, a new dance was being developed, which was different from any previous dances. It would become known as the Lindy Hop, and later as the Jitterbug. The Lindy Hop was the original form of swing dance and is an eight-count dance based partly on the Charleston and the Breakaway, with influences from other dance styles including those of jazz. Smooth Lindy would develop soon after the birth of Lindy Hop, and these two styles would give rise to various other dances.

Lindy Hop's birthplace was the Savoy Ballroom in Harlem. On 26 March 1926, the Savoy opened its doors and would soon become the epicentre of the Lindy Hop world. The Savoy, the first racially integrated ballroom, was an immediate success with its block-long, 4,000-person-capacity dance floor, and a raised double bandstand. Nightly dancing attracted most of the best dancers in the New York area. Stimulated by the presence of great dancers and the best bands, music at the Savoy was largely hot jazz and swing jazz. Lindy Hoppers competed in massive dance contests every week as two big bands (one on each end of the dance floor) played. The very best dancers formed a dance troupe called Whitey's Lindy Hoppers who performed shows until World War II.

On 4 July 1928, the 18th day of a dance marathon at the Marathon Casino, the NYC Board Of Health finally closed down the event. Four of the original 80 couples were left standing. Savoy star "Shorty" George Snowden (number 7) and his partner shared the prize with the other three couples.

Earlier, with the event in full swing, people could post a small cash prize with the MC for a brief mini-contest among the survivors. This was the backdrop for Shorty's spontaneous throw-out breakaway and a flash footwork improvisation which captured media attention. "What are you doing with your feet?" asked the *Fox Movietone News* interviewer. "The Lindy Hop," replied Shorty George in reference to Charles A. Lindbergh (aka "Lindy") who had the previous year "hopped" the Atlantic, landing on 21 May 1927. The Lindy Hop was officially christened.

The Lindy Hop is the authentic Afro-Euro-American swing dance. It is an unashamedly joyful dance, with a solid, flowing style that closely reflects its music, from the late 1920s hot jazz to the early 1940s big band swing. Just as jazz combines European and African musical origins, the Lindy Hop draws on African and European dance traditions. The embracing hold and the turns are from Europe; the solid, earthy body posture is from Africa but with an American-created partner breakaway. The dance evolved along with the new swing music, based on earlier dances such as the Charleston by the black people of Harlem, New York. Two main styles of Lindy Hop developed during the swing era: Frankie Manning's "Savoy Style" and Dean Collins' "Hollywood Style". During the 1940s and 1950s and later, other styles of swing dance would evolve out of the Lindy Hop, including West Coast Swing, East Coast Swing, Rockabilly Swing, Boogie Woogie, Ballroom Jive, Balboa, Shag, Bop, Imperial, Whip and Push.

Above: 1940's style – the Lindy Hop.

ONE O'CLOCK JUMP

Swing was the music that defined a generation, so much so that the 1930s and 40s are often referred to as the swing era. Its smooth, up-tempo, expansive sound was a rejection of earlier jazz styles. In a sense, swing released the restraints placed on musicians by early jazz by simply letting the music run its course.

Major changes that marked the introduction of swing included the use of a more freely flowing rhythmic scheme, using four beats to a bar instead of two beats, which was common in New Orleans jazz. Another change was the common use of riffs, or short melodic ideas, that were used repetitiously in call-and-response patterns between instrumental sections of a band.

Swing abandoned smaller groups like trios and quartets in favour of much larger groups of 15 or more members. Though it was nothing more than just a style of jazz, swing broke all the rules: it was loose, free, and completely modern. However, it is overly simplistic to group together all swing and big band music, as within the genre many different rhythmic and harmonic styles flourished. There were the hot bands, with their hard-driving sound, such as those of Benny Goodman, Count Basie and Duke Ellington, but there were also those that put less emphasis on improvisation and more on feeling and emotion. These were called sweet bands. Among these sweet bands were the Glenn Miller, Freddy Martin, and Wayne King orchestras. Not all big bands were swing bands either. In fact, many big bands experimented with styles such as bebop and cool jazz, like Count Basie, who was nicknamed "The Red Bank Flash".

"Music is your own experience, your own thoughts, your wisdom. If you don't live it, it won't come out of your horn. They teach you there's a boundary line to music. But, man, there's no boundary line to art."

CHARLIE PARKER

Above: The Glen Miller 'sweet' band of the swing era.

BIOGRAPHY:
Count Basie

Born 21 August 1904 in Red Bank, New Jersey
Theme song: 'One O'Clock Jump'

William Basie started playing piano with the Benny Moten band in Kansas City. After Moten's death, Basie became the new leader. In 1935, after starting a small group, he signed up for a broadcast with the Reno Club's experimental radio station, W9XBY. It was on one of those broadcasts that he was transformed into "Count" Basie.

Basie wins the prize for the most swinging band of the 1930s and 1940s. A lot of the bands coming up during this period were moving toward flashy effects, with tough arrangements and speed-driven soloists. In contrast, Basie's orchestra was made up of musicians that just seemed content to swing out, sometimes for hours on end, in their Kansas City tradition. They did not write much down and most of the early recordings are "head arrangements", basically extended variations that turned into songs.

On its first trip to New York, Basie's band was considered rough for big city tastes as they played too loud and too long. By the late 1930s, however, it had gained a nearly fanatical audience. Basie's rhythm section was known as "The All-American Rhythm Section", by both the public and other musicians alike and consisted of Walter Page on bass, Freddie Green on the archtop guitar and Jo Jones, master of the hi-hat, on drums. The band had an incredible brass section with the solid trumpet skills of Buck Clayton and the twin tenors of Herschel Evans and Lester Young. Young was a soloist who became a major influence on later bebop masters. As a young man, the Count would play the piano using the usual number of notes for any given tune. In later years, his musical acumen became so keen, that he could actually capture the very essence of a tune in just a single fistful of notes. He became a true "poet" of the piano.

The basic style of the Count's band usually consisted of a "riff" that could be played either thematically, or behind the soloists. Outstanding examples of this riff style can be heard in the Count's 'One O'Clock Jump', Glenn Miller's 'In the Mood' and also in Woody Herman's 'Woodchopper's Ball'. This "riff" style is the basis of what is known as swing.

Basie's touring diminished in the early 1970s and after he suffered a heart attack in 1976 he made only special appearances. The Count died on 26 April 1984.

Perhaps the most famous of all bands during the swing era was the orchestra led by Glen Miller. This orchestra above all others defined the swing sound not just in America but for the whole world.

Above: William "Count" Basie.

Glenn Miller

Born 1 March 1904 in Clarinda, Indiana
Theme song: 'Moonlight Serenade'

Early on in his musical career, Glenn Miller had worked at a variety of musical jobs and played a jazz trombone. He was a sideman in travelling "road bands" as well as a member of New York theatrical "pit bands". He also authored a significant quantity of arrangements and original tunes including his theme song 'Moonlight Serenade'.

Miller always felt that he was not a very good trombonist, certainly not on a par with the likes of Tommy Dorsey or Jack Teagarden. In reality, he played a reasonably "hot" slide trombone, and can be heard in the Pollack orchestra, and the original Dorsey Brothers band of the early 1930s but after he achieved fame he rarely soloed. In the mid-to-late 1930s, Miller also was the backbone — and often, the behind-the-scenes leader and arranger — of bands that were fronted by John Scott Trotter and cowboy actor/singer Smith Ballew. He had been greatly influenced by Jimmie Lunceford's style of musicianship and was also a disciplinarian who drilled his orchestra to perfection.

In 1937 he formed his own orchestra whose "sound" was like that of many other bands of the time, although they had a few hotel bookings, radio dates and some recordings for Brunswick. After an engagement at the Raymor Ballroom in Bridgeport, Connecticut, Miller returned to New York and disbanded the group in January 1938. The band included Pee Wee Erwin and Charlie Spivak on trumpets, Hal MacIntyre and Jerry Jerome on saxophones, Irving Fazola on clarinet, and Miller's close friend, Chummy MacGregor, on piano.

By March/April, 1938, Miller had formed a new orchestra, which was to become the core of the Miller band and key to the Miller "sound", that of the clarinet lead, with tenor saxophone (or saxophones) playing the same melody one octave lower than the clarinet. MacGregor was still on piano, Hal MacIntyre played alto, Tex Beneke arrived as tenor sax, Willie Schwartz came in on clarinet and Ray Eberle was the male singer.

In June, 1938, Miller was performing at the Paradise Restaurant in New York City, and his music was piped to the nation via NBC radio broadcasts. After trying several female "songbirds", Miller hired Marion Hutton, the sister of Hollywood star Betty Hutton, around September 1938. By early 1939, the band was under recording contract to Bluebird (RCA) and booked for a long stay at the Meadowbrook Ballroom in Cedar Grove, New Jersey. By mid-1939, they were performing at the Glen Island Casino in New Rochelle, New York and their music continued to be broadcast over NBC, adding further to their popularity.

Above: On trombone, the legendary Glenn Miller.

On 6 October 1939, the Miller band, along with other orchestras, performed at Carnegie Hall. Their popularity growing, the band launched their *Chesterfield Show* broadcasts in December and began a long stay at the Cafe Rouge of the Hotel Pennsylvania in New York City in January 1940. The Modernaires vocal group came on board in early 1941. By March, the orchestra was in Hollywood doing the filming and soundtrack work for the 20th Century Fox film *Sun Valley Serenade*. It starred Miller, the band, skater Sonja Henie and John Payne. A year later, they were back at Fox for their second film, *Orchestra Wives*, which featured George Montgomery, Ann Rutherford and Carole Landis. Billy May and Ray Anthony, who would later go on to lead their own orchestras, were in the Miller trumpet section. During this period, May was doing a lot of arrangements for the band, including his beautiful orchestration for the opening of 'Serenade in Blue'.

One of the songs from the movies, 'Chattanooga Choo Choo', became the first million-seller. RCA Victor presented Miller with a gold-plated version of the record to commemorate the event and gold records were used to recognise million-sellers from then on. When World War II erupted, Miller gave a series of Saturday afternoon performances at various military camps across the country. These were broadcast as the *Sunset Serenade* shows, the first of which was aired on 30 August 1941.

By 1942, the band was at the peak of their success and popularity, and Miller was definitely making substantial profits from recordings, broadcasts and personal appearances. Miller felt a need to do more for the United States war effort and joined the military. The last engagement of Miller's civilian orchestra was on 26 September 1942 at the Central theatre in Passaic, New Jersey, only four and a half years after it started. They performed their most popular songs, including 'In the Mood', 'Moonlight Cocktail', 'I've Got a Gal in Kalamazoo' and played their 'Moonlight Serenade' theme for the last time.

Sadly Major Glenn Miller died in an airplane crash during WW2. Tex Benecke, his first chair sax-man and vocalist took over the band and they toured far and wide, remaining active for many more years in honour of their first leader.

If Benny Goodman was "The King of Swing" then Paul Whiteman was "The King of Jazz".

Above: the hugely popular Glen Miller Orchestra.

Above: Paul Whiteman, the "King of Jazz", according to a musical instrument company.

BIOGRAPHY:
Paul Whiteman

Born 1887 in Colorado
Theme song: 'Rhapsody in Blue'

Paul Whiteman's father, Wilberforce, was the superin-tendent for musical education in the Denver public school system. As such, he was responsible for develop-ing the musical talents of a great many other young-sters, including Jimmie Lunceford. In 1915 Whiteman, a then-viola player out of the San Francisco Symphony Orchestra, was captivated by the sound of jazz and filled with ambition to play it. Whiteman joined the John Tait Band. He was fired after just one day when it was discovered that he could not play jazz, although he was to meet Ferde Grofé, Tait's pianist on that eventful day.

In 1917 the US Army turned Whiteman down because of his weight, but the US Navy picked him up as a band-leader. In 1918 he formed his first band, the Paul Whiteman Orchestra, for the Fairmont Hotel in San Francisco, and played dates in and around LA before set-tling in the Hotel Alexandria in LA at the end of 1919. His pianist was Ferde Grofé, who was Whiteman's own age, and who had also been a viola player with the LA Symphony Orchestra. before con-centrating on the piano. After three years as pianist with Paul, Grofé became the band's full-time arranger/composer. Other pianists who followed Grofé were Roy Bargy, Lennie Hayton and Ray Turner.

In 1920, his band began their Victor recordings and he achieved national fame. In 1923, a musical instrument company named him "King of Jazz" as part of a promo-tional event, and this title would remain with Whiteman forever.

Whiteman's orchestra achieved firsts in many areas. It was the first to popularise arrangements and use full reed and brass sections. It was the first big band to play in vaudeville, travel to Europe, use a female singer (Mildred Bailey who was Al Rinker's sister). And it was the first to feature a vocal trio, known as the Rhythm Boys, consisting of Al Rinker, Harry Barris and Bing Crosby, who all got their breaks in this band. Virtually every musician of note played in Whiteman's orchestra at one time or another. In 1924, Whiteman introduced George Gershwin's 'Rhapsody in Blue' at the historic Aeolian Hall Concert, in New York City. Even though his band never ever played "jazz", he did often employ some of the very best jazzmen of the day, including the leg-endary Bix Beiderbecke on cornet. The popularity of his recorded music endures to this day, as does the music of the leg-endary Dorsey Brothers.

The Dorsey Brothers

Jimmy Dorsey born 29 February 1904
Tommy Dorsey born 19 November 1905
Jimmy's theme song: 'Contrasts'
Tommy's theme song: 'I'm getting sentimental over you'

Both Jimmy and Tommy Dorsey were taught music by their father, originally a coal miner, but who later became the leader of the Elmore Band and then a music teacher. From an early age Jimmy studied the slide trumpet and cornet and by the age of seven was playing cornet in his father's band.

In September 1913, he appeared briefly (two days) in a New York theatre variety act with J. Carson McGee's King Trumpeters. In 1915 he switched to the saxophone. Around 1917, Jimmy and his brother Tommy formed a group called Dorsey's Novelty Six that later became Dorsey's Wild Canaries. The group found work in Baltimore where they also became one of the first jazz groups to broadcast. Following their Baltimore residency, they disbanded and the two brothers joined Billy Lustig's Scranton Sirens and made their first recordings of 'Three O'Clock In The Morning' and 'Fate'.

Throughout the 1920s, Jimmy Dorsey played with the orchestras of Paul Whiteman, Harry Thies, Vincent Lopez, Ray Miller, Red Nichols and Jean Goldkette. In September 1924, Jimmy was playing with the California Ramblers, and from 1925 on did much freelance radio and recording. In 1930 Jimmy joined the Ted Lewis Orchestra which included a tour of Europe. He left Lewis in August 1930, returned to the USA, and found work with the orchestras of Andre Kostelanetz, Jacques Renard, Lennie Hayton, Fred Rich, Rudy Vallee, Victor Young and Rubinoff.

Although the Dorsey Brothers had been leading orchestras during the very late 1920s and early 1930s they were not full-time. In the spring of 1934, however, they formed a full-time band. At first they toured outside of New York City, but in July 1934 made their official debut at the Sands Point Beach Club in Long Island City, New York. The Dorsey Brothers band played more dates in and around the New York City area, including appearances at the Palisades Amusement Park on the shore of the Hudson River, and the Riviera Club near the George Washington Bridge. In May 1935, their band was booked into the famous Glen Island Casino in New Rochelle, a suburb of New York, the location of the infamous Tommy Dorsey incident. Brother Tommy had called for some number and was giving the band the tempo. Jimmy made a rude comment and Tommy just picked up his trombone, played a "razz" note and walked off the stage, right in the middle of the performance. It was then that the Jimmy Dorsey Orchestra was born. All of the sidemen stayed with Jimmy as the leader, and the band assumed Jimmy's name in place of that of the Dorsey Brothers.

Above: The Dorsey Brothers, Tommy (top) and Jimmy (bottom).

Bob Eberle, Ray Eberle's brother, who had come into the band just prior to the break-up of the brothers, also stayed with Jimmy and he was the vocalist on the orchestra's 1940 recording of 'The Breeze and I' which became a million-seller.

The 1938 the Jimmy Dorsey Orchestra., with Bob Eberle on vocals, consisted of Jimmy, Milt Yaner, Herbie Hamyer, Leonard Whitney and Charles Frazier on sax-ophones; Ralph Muzzillo, Shorty Sherock and Don Mattison on trumpets; Bobby Byrne and Sonny Lee on trombones; Ray McKinley on drums; Roc Hilman on guitar; Jack Ryan on bass and Freddy Slack on piano.

Above: Tommy Dorsey's orchestra.

In 1939 they were joined by a second vocalist, Helen O'Connell. The two vocalists were heard in more of the band's biggest hit recordings, like 'Amapola', 'Green Eyes' in 1941. The 1941 hit 'Maria Elena' featured just Eberle. In 1942, Eberle and O'Connell teamed up on the Jimmy Dorsey hit recording of 'Tangerine'. The 1943 recording of 'Besame Mucho' with Bob Eberle was another hit record. The same year, Helen O'Connell left the band. Jimmy also appeared in a number of films such as *That Girl From Paris, Shall We Dance, The Fleet's In, I Dood It, Lost In A Harem, 4 Jacks and a Jeep* and the 1947 biopic *The Fabulous Dorseys*.

After the somewhat acrimonious split Tommy went on to form his own band, taking over the Joe Haymes band that was then playing at the Hotel McAlpin. He made his first recordings in September 1935. A few months later, while playing the Blue Room of the Hotel Lincoln (NYC), he instituted several personnel changes. He brought in drummer Dave Tough and tenor saxman Bud Freeman. He then raided Bert Block's band (a local New York City band) for trumpeter Joe Bauer, vocalist Jack Leonard and Odd Stordahl, an arranger. These three also functioned as a vocal trio called The Three Esquires. Odd Stordahl was later to become Axel Stordahl, who did many of the arrangements for Frank Sinatra.

Tommy Dorsey made his name as the "Sentimental Gentleman" of swing, featuring a heavy vibrato on his trombone that set the standard for sweet bands to come. The Tommy Dorsey band of 1938, with Edythe Wright and Jack Leonard on vocals, consisted of Hymie Schertzer, Babe Russin, Johnny Mince, Dean Kincaide and Fred Stuice on saxophones; Charlie Spivak, Yank Lawson and Lee Castaldo on trumpets; Tommy, Moe Zudecoff, Les Jenkins, Elmer Smithers on trombones; Maurice Purtill on drums; Carmen Mastren on guitar; Gene Traxler on bass and Howard Smith on piano.

In the 1940s, he proved that he also had his ear to the ground as regards public taste, featuring the "hot" arrangements of Sy Oliver (Jimmie Lunceford Orchestra) alongside his moody trademark numbers. With the addition of maverick drummer Buddy Rich and the young vocalist Frank Sinatra, Dorsey's later bands presented the best of both worlds: a band that could keep the Jitterbuggers out of their seats

with Rich's drum features but also charm the romantics with Frank's ballad interpretations. This hot-and-cool tension was evident within the band itself, with Rich, Sinatra and Dorsey constantly at odds with one another while on tour.

During World War II, Tommy amplified his band's sound by adding a string section. At the end of the war, he dropped the strings and added more horns, which gave the band a bigger sound, with Bill Finegan as the arranger. Throughout his career, Tommy sometimes played his trombone with that velvet tone for which he was so well known, and at other times manifested the rough, husky tone of his Jazz roots.

The two brothers would not speak to each other or appear together again for many years, although they finally did reconcile their differences. Although Jimmy had worked with his own big bands during the late 1940s and early 1950s, from the spring of 1953 he rejoined the Tommy Dorsey Orchestra, which was then billed as The Fabulous Dorseys Orchestra. Jimmy later became the sole leader after Tommy died in 1956. In the last year of his life, ill health forced Jimmy to hand over leadership to Lee Castle.

In 1957, Jimmy died of cancer.

Another huge name during the swing era was Artie Shaw.

Above: Young Frank Sinatra.

Above: Artie Shaw.

BIOGRAPHY:

Artie Shaw

Born 23 May 1910 in New York City, New York
Theme song: 'Nightmare'

Artie Shaw was raised in Connecticut and took up the alto sax when he was 12. A few years later he was already playing in local bands. After leaving home at the age of 15 for a job in Kentucky, which never materialised, he had to work in travelling bands to get back home. He is known to have worked with Don "Johnny" Cavallaro in New Haven and Florida, following which he travelled to Cleveland, Ohio, where he worked in the Merle Jacobs and Joe Cantor bands.

In 1926, Artie switched to the clarinet and spent the following three years in Cleveland working on and off as arranger/musical director for the Austin Wylie band. He also doubled on tenor sax and clarinet while playing with the Irving Aronson Commanders. At the end of 1929 Artie moved to New York. While waiting for his local musicians' union card, he played with pianist Willie "The Lion" Smith at Pod's and Jerry's, a Harlem night spot. Often sitting in at after-hours sessions at local clubs, he earned a reputation as a technically brilliant clarinettist. He recorded as a sideman with various jazz bands, including Teddy Wilson, backing Billie Holiday, and others such as Vincent Lopez, Paul Specht, Roger Wolfe Kahn and finally with Red Nichols at the Park Central Hotel in 1931.

In late 1931, he worked in the Fred Rich band for a year and then re-joined the Roger Wolfe Kahn band for a year-long tour during 1933. After this, Artie freelanced in New York recording studios and clubs.

In 1934, he took a break from the music business to run a farm in the Buck's County area of Pennsylvania, after which he returned to freelancing in New York.

In May 1936, Shaw formed a small band for a booking at the Imperial theatre. The gig was so successful that he was able to obtain financial backing to form a larger group, with regular dance band instrumentation, for a recording contract and a Boston debut, although it was rather short-lived. In April 1937, he formed a more conventional big band that was an immediate success, mainly due to the fine melodic arrangements of Jerry Gray. This band made several recordings including the hugely successful 'Begin The Beguine' which propelled his band to the forefront of leading dance bands. This band had such sidemen as Johnny Best on trumpet; Les Robinson and Georgie Auld on reeds, Tony Pastor on tenor sax and Cliff Leeman on drums. Later on drummer Buddy Rich would join.

Pastor, Hank Freeman and Ronny Perry on saxophones; Johnny Best, Claude Bowen and Chuck Peterson on trumpets; Russell Brown, Harry Rogers and George Aruson on trombones; Cliff Leeman on drums; Sid Weiss on bass; Al Avola on guitar and Les Burness on piano. Owing to record company contractual problems, Billie only made one recording with Shaw: 'Any Old Time'.

In the summer of 1939, he was absent from the band for a tonsillectomy and in November he disbanded the orchestra and went to Mexico. On his return he featured in the Fred Astaire-Paulette Goddard film *Second Chorus*. This film brought him another hit record in 'Frenesi'. He then formed a band that had both a string section and a band within a band, the Gramercy Five. This big band had such sidemen as Billy Butterfield and Jack Jenney on trumpets, Nick Fatool on drums and Johnny Guarneri on piano. Guarneri also switched from the piano to the harpsichord, giving the Gramercy Five a very distinctive sound. A number of very successful recordings followed including 'Concerto for Clarinet', 'Summit Ridge Drive' and 'Special Delivery Stomp'. However, Shaw's dislike of life in the public eye again caused him to disband. He later formed another big band, although this folded when America entered World War II.

In 1938, Billie Holiday sang with the band but she left after a succession of disagreeable incidents caused by racial discrimination which was then prevalent in New York's hotels and radio stations. The actual band when Billie was with him consisted of Les Robinson, Tony

Above: Artie Shaw featured in the Fred Astaire-Paulette Goddard film Second Chorus.

In 1942, now a member of the US Navy, Shaw hand-picked some sidemen and formed a band that toured the South Pacific warzone.

In February 1944, he received a medical discharge and formed a new band that featured sidemen such as Roy "Little Jazz" Eldridge on trumpet; Barney Kessel, Dodo Marmarosa and Chuck Gentry on reeds; Stan Fishelson, and other top musicians. Again this band was short-lived. Through the remainder of the 1940s, Shaw formed other bands only to break them up within a few months of their formation.

In the late 1940s, he began studying the classical guitar. He also began developing a career as a writer. In February 1949, he guested at New York's Carnegie Hall with the National Symphony Orchestra and in the spring of that year had a short gig at New York's Bop City. In September 1949, he was again touring with a big band, continuing into the early 1950s. In late 1953, he re-formed a very short-lived Gramercy Five. After this, he once again tried his hand at dairy farming in Skekomeko, New York.

By the mid-1950s, he had retired from music and spent much of his time writing. In 1955, he moved to Gerona, Spain, where he remained, as a writer, playing no music until he returned to the US in 1960. At that time, he was married to film actress Evelyn Keyes and they moved to a home in Lakeville, Connecticut, where he continued to write. In the 1980s, Shaw again formed a band, this time under the direction of Dick Johnson. The 1985 film documentary *Time Is All You've Got* traced his career in some

detail. Artie's capacity to form and disband many orchestras was echoed in his personal life. In all, he had eight wives, among them Lana Turner, Ava Gardner, Kathleen Windsor, Doris Dowling and the aforementioned Evelyn Keyes.

Shaw's erratic bandleading career and his erratic personal life precluded his ever reaching the same level of musicianship as, say, Benny Goodman. Nevertheless, he always had a very delightful and musical band and, through his frequent hiring of black musicians such as Oran "Hot Lips" Page, Billie Holiday and Roy "Little Jazz" Eldridge, helped to bring down racial barriers.

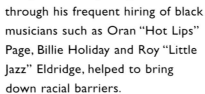

Above: Billie Holiday, who briefly sang with Artie Shaw.

SOCIETY BANDS

There were many different types of orchestras during the big band era. Some specialised in playing swing, while others played jazz. From the very earliest days of popular music, there was one group of bands that came to be known as "society" orchestras. Back in the 1930s and 1940s, everyone danced whether fleet of foot or clumsy. When the music started, people got up from their tables and started to dance, and so it followed that all bands came to be called dance bands. Some bands featured "sweet" music and some were "hot", but most of them played both styles.

Benny Goodman, acclaimed as the "King of Swing", was in essence the leader of a dance band. True, it was a dance band that leaned more toward the "hot" rather than the "sweet". Paralleling Goodman, but on the other side of the fence, were orchestras such as those of Vincent Lopez, Hal Kemp, Kay Kyser and Larry Clinton. In fact, the "sweet" bands were, by far, in the majority. People just simply wanted to dance and "society" orchestras catered for that market.

There were two types of society bands. The first were essentially band agencies. These agencies would have several different orchestras playing in various places in one night, under the same name. For example, 15 different Ben Selvin bands could be playing on the same evening at 15 different social events but all were billed as the Ben Selvin Orchestra. The best-known of these bands went under the names of Emil Coleman, Meyer Davis, Ernie Hecksher and Lester Lanin. Many of these had been formed in the early 1920s and catered especially for debutante balls and other upper-crust social gatherings.

The second group consisted of single-entity, independent bands who were usually booked into a local hotel where they played dance music for the patrons. From these performances they would often pick up gigs for society gatherings. The best-known of these outfits were those of Eddie Duchin, Anson Weeks, Ted Straeter, Gray Gordon and Shep Fields. Most of the band members were session musicians who backed up the orchestra leader. The best example of this is the Eddie Duchin Orchestra; Duchin was a "society darling". His band was always in demand for private balls and galas as well as for playing hotels.

This type of band used gimmicks to give them a recognisable sound and so make them stand out from other dance bands. Gray Gordon developed a sound using temple blocks as his trademark and was widely known as Gray Gordon and his Tick Tock Rhythm. Shep Fields had one of his sidemen blow bubbles through a straw in a glass of water, and his band came to be called Shep Fields and His Rippling Rhythm. However, in spite of all the gimmicks, it was the dances themselves that were important.

DANCING IN THE SWING ERA

Many African-American dancers in 1920s were able to teach the whites how to Lindy, which allowed them to make a good living in what was a particularly racist and therefore difficult period. There was a great deal of competition among some African-American dancers, and so at the dances they would stick paper advertisements to their backs, with either a phone number or a studio name written on them. Anyone who liked the style of the dancer could then contact them in order to take lessons. Through this type of competition, the dancers would start to perform more wild and crazy stuff to get the attention of the spectators.

Dance contests became more and more outrageous. In the 1930s a dancer named Frankie Manning added the first air step (lifts/flips) to the Lindy. These and other air steps, or aerials, had been done for years in other dances by professional club entertainers, but supposedly had not yet been done in the Lindy. When interviewed, Frankie described how his first aerial took place. He and his partner were practising for a dance contest to try and beat the then "King", Shorty George Snowden, at the Savoy Ballroom. They tried out a back flip they had seen and it worked and so they performed it in the contest, thereby beating George Snowden.

Films such as *Hellzapoppin* and *A Day at the Races*, as well as *Malcolm X* and *Swing Kids* show seemingly reckless aerials, often done at very fast musical tempos. Far from being just acrobatic antics, aerials are in fact smooth, extremely precise, and done in time with the music. They require a high degree of expertise and are not danced socially, but only as spectacle, if only inside a protective ring of spectators, called a "jam circle".

In the early 1930s, Hubert "Whitey" White was the head bouncer at the Savoy and took the opportunity to make some money by forming a group called Whitey's Hopping Maniacs, later known as Whitey's Lindy Hoppers. The only competition he had was from Shorty George and his dancers, who were doing most of the exhibitions and shows in the ballrooms and the clubs such as the Cotton Club. Whitey held auditions and picked some dancers to start his group. This group established the form of Lindy Hop we know today. During the Lindy Hoppers' reign, the Lindy was to take on a newer, more sophisticated and cleaner form. The Hoppers travelled all over the world performing in many exhibitions, films and stage shows.

Dean Collins learned to dance the Lindy Hop at the Savoy, but developed his own unique style. His style was slower and smoother and he brought it to Los Angeles in the early 1930s. Collins' style of swing dancing, often called "smooth Lindy", would be used in many Hollywood films, thus the style came to be referred to as "Hollywood". In San Diego, California, Smooth Lindy later slowed even further, taking on many more six-beat moves and a very strict slotted motion for the lady. This became known as West Coast Swing and is more usually danced to blues rather than swing music. It is the official state dance of California. "Jitterbug" was originally a slang term for those who drank a lot of alcohol, known as "jitter". However, in the mid-1930s, the Lindy Hop started to be called the Jitterbug when Cab Calloway introduced a tune in 1934 entitled "Jitterbug". Also the pilot after whom the

Lindy Hop was named , Charles Lindbergh, became ostracised by many Americans as he opposed the voluntary entry of the USA into World War II.

The term Jitterbug would eventually be applied to all styles of swing dancing over the years that followed and the term Lindy Hop would almost be forgotten.

LOS AMERICANOS

Above: Dancing the Cuban Conga in the 1940s.

In the history of big bands, one of the most important factors was the influence of the slave trade. The slaves brought with them the primal beats and rhythms of their African culture. In Cuba, for instance, even though the Spanish slave masters forced the slaves to adopt Catholicism, on saints' days they would secretly worship their own tribal spirits called Orisha who were endowed with human qualities. Widely known as Santeria, this cult of the saints was derived from the Yoruban culture and religion of what is now Nigeria.

When the slave masters outlawed the use of drums, the early slaves took to hitting the sides of salted codfish boxes with their bare hands. This eventually led to the development of the conga drum and soon both the conga and rumba rhythms were being tapped out, both of them now essential components of Cuban music.

It is interesting to note the differences between Cuban songs and American jazz forms. Caribbean and Cuban songs usually feature a vocalist and a 3- or 4-member chorus, while the blues and jazz which developed in New Orleans at much the same time use a call-and-response system, usually between the vocalist and instrumentalist or, in swing bands, between the instrumental soloist and the band.

Modern Latin-American music consists of many different rhythms, such as the mambo, cha-cha-cha, conga, rumba and merengue, which are all marketed as "salsa". Latin-American music is a mixture of the formerly suppressed African culture and the music of Spain with its use of stringed instruments. As its popularity widened, Latin music diversified into two distinct types; it either expanded to the big band sound or contracted into a small combo style that was more flexible for jazz. In both, the common denominator is a hard-driving percussive dance rhythm. In the history of Latin-American music, a key moment occurred on 8 August 1928 when the Cuban troubadour Miguel Matamoro formed his own group called El Trio Matamoros.

Other early pioneers were trumpeter Lazaro Herrera, who founded the National Sextet of Ignacio Pineiro, a rumba-based group who made the then new urban sound popular. Arsenio Rodriguez, who was responsible for bringing the Latin sound to New York, added piano and several trumpets to the band's instrumentation.

In 1937, the innovative mambo rhythm was introduced. This was first played at a fast tempo but then was slowed down to allow for the sensual and romantic movements of the ballroom dancers. Perez Prado was the bandleader who became known as "the Mambo King" for his role in its development.

Mario Bauza was another of the major Latin music innovators. In 1940, along with his brother-in-law Machito he founded his Afro-Cuban Jazz Orchestra. In 1950 Tito Puente, born in the East Harlem section of New York, put together his first mambo band for an engagement at La Casa del Mambo, then a popular club on Broadway at 53rd Street. In the late 1950s, Tito was instrumental in bringing the flute and violin music of the Cuban Charanga to public attention. Accordingly the "cha-cha-cha" rhythm became a global favourite of dancers everywhere.

Two singular events caused the music to fall from public favour: the Communist revolution in Cuba and the advent of Beatlemania. However, the large Latin community in the United States kept the music alive and it is still a vibrant musical force today. In common with other popular musical forms, salsa has hybridised into other styles and has also taken on new subject matter. In the 1960s the Joe Cuba Sextet developed a hybrid pop-salsa style called the boogaloo. Bandleader Willie Colon, along with his vocalist Hector Lavoe, known as the bad boys of salsa, brought a tough and streetwise style to the music, while Ruben Blades introduced a political slant and social protest.

In common with so many other pop styles, salsa, or more accurately Latin-American music, has become increasingly protective of its roots as a populist Caribbean dance music, and this has enabled it to maintain its thriving form. Xavier Cugat was the man who was responsible for the introduction of Latin music during the big band era, both to the US and to the world.

BIOGRAPHY:

Xavier Cugat - The Rumba King

Born 1 January 1900 in Tirona, Catalonia, Spain
Theme song: 'My Shawl'

When Xavier Cugat was three years old his family moved to Havana, Cuba. A local instrument maker gave him a violin and Cugat proceeded to learn music. He was an adept student and, in 1912, became first violinist with the Orchestra of the Teatro Nacional in Havana. He continued his violin studies in Berlin, later playing in various orchestras. Enrico Caruso, the famous opera singer, discovered Cugat and brought him to America. In the US Cugat first became Caruso's accompanist, but was soon playing as a sideman with bands such as Vincent Lopez and Phil Harris. During the day he also worked as a newspaper cartoonist for the *Los Angeles Times*. He was so good that his caricatures of celebrities often appeared at exhibitions.

In the mid-1920s, he formed the Latin American Band and played at many of the local Los Angeles clubs. In 1928 he got his big break when his band secured a booking at the prestigious Cocoanut Grove in Los Angeles. In the early 1930s, his orchestra started a rumba boom with their hit version of 'El Manicero', and it was for this that he became known as "the Rumba King". All through the 1940s, Cugat's band was extremely popular and it became the house orchestra at New York's elite Waldorf-Astoria Hotel. The high-society guests loved Cugat and his band and they became the most famous Latin-American orchestra of the 1940s, resulting in the band's appearance in a number of Hollywood films. Cugat also composed film music, albeit largely uncredited, including *In Gay Madrid* (1930), *White Zombie* (1932), *The Man From Monterey* (1933), *The Americano* (1955), *Tempo di villeggiatura* (1956), *Donatella* (1956), *Das Feuerschiff* (1962) and *Holiday in Mexico* (1946).

He retired from music in 1971 after suffering a stroke and died in 1990, having returned to Spain.

Above: Xavier Cugat, the "King of Rumba".

BIOGRAPHY:

Tito Puente

Born 20 April 1923 in New York

Tito Puente's first dream was to become a dancer. An accident which tore his ankle tendon forced him to change his career path permanently and instead he began to study the piano. In 1945, after he had been discharged from the US Naval Reserves, he took formal lessons at New York's Juilliard School of Music. Whilst there he played with a number of Latin bandleaders including Pupi Campo, Noro Morales and Machito. In 1949 he formed the Piccadilly Boys which eventually became the Tito Puente Orchestra. Band members included Willie Bobo, Ray Barretto, Johnny Pacheco and Mongo Santamaria.

In the 1950s, Puente did a lot of "crossover" work and infused the American big bands with a Latin "feel". He helped the cha-cha-cha sound into the mainstream by transforming the old Cuban violin and flute Charanga music into a big-band reeds-and-brass sound. He continued playing "crossover" into the 1960s by interpreting bossa novas and Broadway show tunes in a Latin way.

In the 1970s, Tito Puente and his Latin Percussion Ensemble toured Europe. He recorded with Cal Tjader and Ray Barretto for Fantasy and Atlantic records. In the 1980s he won a number of awards including two Grammys, one in 1983 for his *Tito Puente and his Latin Ensemble on Broadway* album and one in 1985 for *Mambo Diablo*. The jazz pianist George Shearing was featured on it playing 'Lullaby of Birdland'. In 1992 he made an appearance in the film *The Mambo Kings*.

Puente died on 2 June 2000 in New York.

Although swing music was really urban music, elsewhere in the country other big bands were filling dance halls with their own variations. This has come to be known as Western Swing.

Above: The Grammy-winning Tito Puente.

TEXAS PLAYBOYS

WESTERN SWING

For most people, the word swing evokes memories of the great big bands that played all over America in the late 1930s to 1950s. To millions of Americans, though, there was another swing: Western Swing.

Western Swing was played in the roadhouses, county fairs and dance halls of small towns throughout Texas and the Oklahoma Lower Great Plains. The people who came to the roadhouses were of course, all "locals" – everyone knew everyone else, friends and neighbours, husbands and wives, all coming to spend some time listening, drinking and dancing their week-ends away.

The term Western Swing was coined in the early 1940s by "Spade" Cooley. Before that, the music had been called everything from Texas Swing to Hillbilly. Cooley was a multi-millionaire who led America's largest swing band. He had his own television show and a large "ranch" on Ventura Boulevard in Los Angeles. Unfortunately in a fit of jealousy he murdered his wife Ella Mae Evans because he believed she was having an affair with Roy Rogers, the cowboy film star. He also forced his daughter to watch. He was sent to prison where eight years later, he died of a coronary.

During the heyday of Western Swing, there were thousands of bands playing all over the American West. Yet it was only a handful of bands, playing predominantly in southern Oklahoma and north-eastern Texas, that had established the genre.

Above: "Spade" Cooley and his Orchestra.

The music was strictly for dancing and included mostly simpler one- and two-step dances with quite a few fox-trots, along with both "cowboy" and "Mexican" waltzes. Usually the bandleader or a small group of the sidemen handled the vocals. The popularity of the leader or vocalist usually determined the band's success. Although the local bands covered the same music that the big city bands were playing, because of the smaller instrumentation and rural style, the music had a different "feel". Rather than a big band sound, it was much more ensemble playing, often with guitar or violin predominating.

String bands fathered the music which we now call Western Swing. These early string bands often consisted of just a mandolin, banjo, a standard six-string guitar, and a four-string tenor guitar, also known as the baritone ukelele. Since microphones were not in wide use, the music largely consisted of instrumental "breakdowns" rather than vocalists who could not be heard properly. In areas where people were too poor or too remote to attend dance halls, then weekend "house parties" would be held. Local bands would perform and people would take it in turns to host the party and invite their neighbours over.

The south-west population consisted of German, Irish, English and French immigrants and the music accordingly represented the area's cultural and economic background. At first the songs and the "hot licks" were passed along between just the neighbourhood musicians. Records were rarely played on the radio stations as the recording companies believed that to do so would affect their sales. This resulted in local bands playing live at radio stations in their vicinity, further compounding the effects of localisation.

Since the music was heard only by people in the station's listening area, the region's musical identity was thus codified. Later, mass marketing of records and improved radio broadcasting made the music and styles of all areas available to musicians all over the West.

From the early 1920s the music which probably best reflected the local ethnicity slowly began to develop into the first "country" music, and ultimately mirrored the music that the urban big bands were playing. It differed from big-band music in that the instrumentation was not the same, and the style was more ensemble playing. Following this same pattern, Western Swing would later develop into bop and then rock 'n' roll.

The development of recording helped break down the racial, religious and social barriers that existed in many areas of life. However, in music, "artificial" boundaries and marketing categories were created such as race records (for black listeners), hillbilly records and Western Swing. On the West Coast the marketing strategy worked very well, but on the more sophisticated East Coast record sales suffered as people did not consider themselves to fit so neatly into the categories.

Probably the best-known of the early Western Swing bands were Milton Brown and his Brownies, and Bob Wills and The Texas Playboys, but there were hundreds more who managed to achieve a modicum of fame even if in just their own regional area. In time, many of the old-timers died, but Western Swing survived. Some of Wills' sidemen, such as his guitarists Tiny Moore and Eldon Shamblin, along with his fiddler Johnny Gimble, continued the Western Swing tradition inspiring future generations. There were such rock-era bands as Commander Cody and his Lost Planet Airmen, Alvan Crow's Pleasant Valley Boys and Asleep At The Wheel.

In addition, there were a great deal of "cross-over" performances. From the jazz world, Stan Kenton recorded with Tex Ritter and Charlie "Yardbird" Parker jammed with Ray Price's Cherokee Cowboys. Jazz vibraphonist Gary Burton and bassist Steve Swallow went into RCA's Nashville recording studios. It worked in reverse, too: jazzmen Hank Garland and drummer Joe Morello had their early band training with Paul Howard's Arkansas Cotton Pickers. Other examples are Benny Golson's Killer Joe coming out of Gimble and The Nashville Pickers; Vassar Clements made two albums of "hillbilly jazz", and Roy Clark formed his own big band.

TERRITORY BANDS

Throughout the 1920s and 1930s, many of the bands with the greatest fame were based in New York. In addition to providing a large pool of musicians for the bands, New York was also the centre of the recording and broadcasting industries. While many of the bands toured extensively, they almost invariably started and ended their tours in New York or the second most important city for music, Chicago. However, there were a great many fine bands that rarely visited New York or Chicago – some never at all. They were based in smaller cities and often employed a fairly stable roster of sidemen. They were known as the territory bands.

Most of the territory bands never achieved national prominence, or worked in the large cities. They were local musicians who toured their area, playing in cafés, ballrooms, touring minstrel and vaudeville shows or at school events. Often, because the personnel of these bands were black, these were the only venues available to them. The "name" big bands made the headlines, but the territory bands disseminated the "sound". In Kansas City, the sound was blue-sy; the south-west had a certain Western Swing sound, and so forth. Overall, they played a rather eclectic mix of classical, ragtime and whatever was the popular music of the day. While their local performances were rarely recorded, their playing was usually happy and lively, and they supplied their audiences with reasonably high-quality entertainment. Many of the territory bands had musicians who were easily the equal to any in the nationally known bands.

Two notable musicians from Kansas City were singer "Big Joe" Turner and pianist Pete Johnson, both Kansas City born and raised. All through the 1920s, Johnson played in various Kansas City cafés including Piney Brown's Sunset Café, where he met Big Joe who was bartending at that time. In 1938, they both went to New York and were appeared in the *Spirituals to Swing* concert at the famed Carnegie Hall.

There were stylistic differences in the music that set Kansas City apart from the rest of the country. Bands in Kansas City, as well as elsewhere in the south-west, relied more heavily on the 12-bar blues structure. They very often used loose "head" arrangements, created in rehearsals or often on the bandstand just before "show" time. These arrangements had lots of "solo space", and utilised a subtle, free-flowing rhythmic drive that tended to show off the soloist to best advantage. This music, closely associated with Kansas City and exemplified by the early Basie band, eventually became part of the great swing era.

Above: Singer "Big Joe" Turner from Kansas City.

Above: the 1950s – 'Rock n Roll is here to stay'.

ROCK 'N' ROLL BANDS

This style of music started in the 1950s. First a form arose called Western Bop, which had its roots in Western Swing but was mixed with Afro-American bebop rhythms. Neither bebop itself nor Western Bop lasted very long. Bebop became unpopular as a musical form, and Western Bop was soon replaced by a slightly different music known first as rockabilly and then as rock 'n' roll.

The 1950s witnessed a historical moment. A gap began to form between the generations. The young rebellious rock 'n' rollers wanted nothing to do with what they called the "square" musicians that had preceded them. In 1951 a Western Swing band called Bill Haley and the Saddlemen, which later became Bill Haley and the Comets arrived on the scene and rock 'n' roll was born.

In the 1960s, the acoustic folk music movement and rockabilly groups kept Western Swing alive. In the 1970s, there was still another resurgence of Western Swing in Austin, Texas. There the music of Bob Wills and Milton Brown was continued by men such as Willie Nelson and Waylon Jennings. The Austin Western Swing scene is alive and well thanks to the annual South by Southwest music festival. In the late 1980s, the band Asleep At The Wheel became hugely successful as a result of the *Austin City Limits* TV show, on which the band played the great Western Swing tunes, often featuring the "old school" players of Western Swing.

Today, the term Western Swing still evokes nostalgic images of cowboys with fiddles, steel guitars and drums touring the countryside in buses and vans. Even though that era has ended, the legacy of those early musicians can still be heard in modern country, rock and pop music.

OVER THE POND

The seeds of the big band culture in British popular music were sown at London's Savoy Hotel. As early as 1916, a group known as the Savoy Quartette had taken up residence there, and remained there until 1920. But the music they played was quite different from the music that was about to sweep the world.

On 7 April 1919, the Original Dixieland Jazz Band opened at the London Hippodrome as part of the Musical Revue *Joy Bells*. Afterwards, they toured variety theatres and finally settled in London's Hammersmith Palais de Danse on 28 November 1919 for a stay of nine months.

In Britain, as in America, it is important to note that dancing was the major impetus in popular music, as evidenced by the popularity of the fox-trot. Hotels made great profits from holding dances and so they ensured that bands had venues in which to play. However, as in the USA, it was the development of radio that established the dance bands as national institutions.

In 1919 Bert Ralton, an American saxophonist, left Art Hickman's band in New York City, went to Havana, Cuba, and formed his own band. Sometime in 1920/1, he arrived in England, and in March 1922 his New York Havana Band played at London's Coliseum theatre. A few months later they opened at the Savoy Hotel as the Savoy Havana Band. On 23 April 1922, they broadcast from a BBC studio, and by the autumn had become the first dance band to have regular, weekly radio broadcasts from the Savoy. In December, Ralton left for Australia and Reginald Batten, the band's violinist, became the leader. By this time, the band had Rudy Vallee on saxophone and Billy Mayerl on piano.

Above: The Original Dixieland Jazz Band.

BIOGRAPHY:

The Savoy Orpheans

The next important date in British dance music occurred in 1923 when Debroy Somers formed his Savoy Orpheans Orchestra. Rudy Vallee was still there, as was Billy Mayerl, and Carroll Gibbons also joined. The Savoy Orpheans were to achieve even greater fame than the Savoy Havana Band. In 1926 Somers left and Cyril Newton became the new leader. In 1927 Carroll Gibbons took over the leadership role and they were joined from the US by trumpeter Frank Guarente, who had had been touring with his New Georgians Orchestra. The two bands remained as the resident orchestras at the Savoy until William de Mornys, the agent for both, withdrew them in 1927 because of the Savoy's refusal to allow them to play other engagements. Carroll Gibbons and Teddy Sinclair became co-leaders of The Original Savoy Orpheans which now included both Max Goldberg and Frank Guarente on trumpet. In 1928, Reg Batten became the leader of The New Savoy Orpheans who included Americans Sylvester Ahola on trumpet and Irving Brodsky on piano.

The Orpheans' history now goes further into the realms of confusion. As the band name guaranteed public interest, a band calling themselves The Original Savoy Orpheans went on tour to Germany, even recording in Berlin. But upon their return they disbanded. In a theatrical production called *Topsy and Eva*, a band calling themselves The New Savoy Orpheans became the pit orchestra but broke up when the production closed. Then, in 1929, Ben Evers got himself

tied up in a legal wrangle when he formed a stage band using the Savoy Orpheans name and was forced to disband. Next Ben Loban, in 1931, and then Jack Hart, in 1932, attempted to revive the name. That same year Carroll Gibbons led a band, resident at the Savoy, called The Savoy Orpheans, but other than the name this band had little in common with any of the previous line-ups. In 1932 the Savoy Hotel, following a legal application, won the exclusive rights to use the name Savoy Orpheans.

During the 1920s and 1930s, American musicians and bands frequently visited England – and London in particular. In the various Orpheans, one could find Frank Guarente, Sylvester Ahola, the Starita brothers and Rudy Vallee. Fred Elizalde's Savoy Hotel Band included Chelsea Quealey, Bobby Davis, Adrian Rollini and Fud Livinston. In 1922 and 1923, the Bar Harbor Orchestra was in England. In 1923 Paul Specht was in residence at London's Lyons Corner House, and in 1925, he played the Kit-Cat Club. In the summer of 1924, the Princeton Triangle Band was playing at the New Princes Restaurant in the Piccadilly Hotel. In late 1925, the Kit-Cat Club brought in the Ted Lewis Orchestra. That same year, both Ted Lewis and Vincent Lopez led their bands at the Hippodrome. In 1926 and 1927, Paul Whiteman toured England. The Paul Specht Canadian Orchestra, fronted by Orville Johnson, played the Kit-Cat Club in 1926, and Abe Lyman was at the same club in 1929, also playing concerts at the London Palladium. Gus Arnheim's band played the Savoy in 1929, while in 1930 Hal Kemp's Orchestra, with Bunny Berigan on trumpet, played at both the Café de Paris and the Coliseum. Two American orchestras managed to stay in England long enough to become "English" orchestras. That is to say, they became an integral part of the English musical tradition. These were the Starita Brothers and Fred Elizalde Orchestras.

While all of the Savoy Orpheans, the New York Savoy Havana Band, and the Fred Elizalde Orchestra are important because they were the real pioneers of British popular music, there were many others. During this same period, many hotels and night clubs were becoming interested in presenting danceable music for their patrons.

BBC radio opened a new world of opportunity to a new group of bands and their leaders. On 24 May 1923, Ben Davis' Carlton Hotel Dance Band was heard on radio, as was Henry Hall's Gleneagles Hotel Orchestra in 1924. In 1925, the BBC carried Jack Payne and his Hotel Cecil Orchestra. On 16 February 1926, the BBC's first house band made its initial broadcast. Called the London Radio Dance Band, it was under the direction of violinist Sidney Firman. In fact this group had previously been resident at London's Cavour Restaurant. In 1928, the BBC decided to form its very own house band, which was called The BBC Dance Orchestra under the direction of Jack Payne. Three years later, it was simply known as Jack Payne and his Orchestra.

BIOGRAPHY:

Jack Payne

Born 22 August 1899 in Leamington Spa, Warwickshire
Theme song: 'Say It With Music'

Jack Payne was an aviator in the Royal Flying Corps during World War I and whilst there he organised dance bands for the corps. After the war he continued working with dance bands and toured with a number of small groups. In 1925, his six-piece band was booked into London's Hotel Cecil. In December of that year, the BBC started remote broadcasts from the Cecil, and Jack enlarged the band to a 10-piece.

Between 1928 and 1932, Payne worked at the BBC as Director of Dance Music. When he left, Henry Hall took over. Payne took the main part of the band with him, although 10 of his sidemen did not follow but instead formed a co-op band called The Barnstormers", using the "tag" "Pleasure Without Payne", until Jack got a legal injunction preventing such use. During this period, Jack Payne's Band was seen in such British-made films as *Symphony In Two Flats* in 1930 and *Sunshine Ahead* in 1936. In 1935, he was in *Say It With Music*, named after his theme song.

Payne's 1936 band successfully toured South Africa. In 1937 Payne disbanded, retired to his stud farm in Buckinghamshire and devoted his time to being an impresario. He had many road shows under his control but frequently ran into legal wrangles that often resulted in litigation.

In 1938 Payne again started touring with a 20-piece band and was on the *Round The Dial* radio show. At the end of 1939 his was the first British band to entertain the troops in France.

In 1941, Billy Ternent stepped down as the BBC's resident Dance Band Director, and Jack Payne again assumed that role until 1946. In the 1950s and 1960s, he worked as a disc Jockey at the BBC. He died in December 1969.

During this period the BBC, due to its stance against commercialisation, did not approve of "song plugging", and even banned giving the title of the songs that bands were playing. Although it would eventually rescind this ruling, the anti-song-plugging mania permeated the British music scene.

Two other orchestras must be mentioned in any overview of the early English dance bands. The Jack Hylton Orchestra recorded prolifically during the early 1920s. Bert Ambrose's Orchestra, too, recorded throughout the 1920s and was already well known; in 1923 his band had been resident at London's Embassy Club.

Above: The BBC Dance Orchestra under the direction of Jack Payne.

BIOGRAPHY:

Bert Ambrose

Born in 1897, London

Towards the end of World War I, Bert Ambrose moved to New York to study and to play the violin in cinema orchestras. After being musical director at the Club de Vingt he was enticed back to London in December 1921, using his cross-Atlantic experience to organise a dance band at Luigi's Embassy Club. In 1922 he briefly returned to New York as musical director at the Clover Gardens but came back to London's Embassy Club.

In 1927 he became musical director at the New Mayfair Hotel and from there Brunswick offered him a recording contract. His band also played at the London Palladium that year. In 1928 he established his orchestra as the most popular in Britain with broadcasts at the BBC. In 1929 he signed a recording deal with Decca, which lasted for the next 20 years.

Both the Decca contract and the reputation of the band's members supported the continual releases of Ambrose material. Band members included Lew Stone, Ted Heath, Bert Barnes, Stanley Black, Kenny Baker, George Shearing and the vocalist Vera Lynn.

Although he was most popular in the 1940s, Ambrose continued organising bands of all sizes and played night clubs and hotels well into the 1950s. He managed other talent acts before retiring from the business in 1956.

Bert Ambrose died in 1973.

Jack Hylton was one of the major pioneers of British dance bands and led what many regard as the premier European show band of the 1920s and 1930s. In 1939, he was even responsible for bringing the comedians Eric Morecambe and Ernie Wise together.

BIOGRAPHY:
Jack Hylton

Born 2 July 1892 in Great Lever, Lancashire
Theme song: 'Oh, Listen To The Band'

Jack Hylton, at only five foot three, became a giant on the British music scene for some four decades. He started his career as "the singing mill boy", playing piano at concert parties and working in a double act with Tommy Handley. He played with the Queen's Dance Orchestra at the Queen's Hall, London. When they first recorded for HMV on 28 May 1921, he was the only member of the band who could read music and before long his name appeared on the label as director of the orchestra. His 1922 band had Bernard Tipping on trombone, Basil Wiltshire on drums, Bert Heath and Jack Raine on trumpet, an unlisted tenor sax, Chappie d'Amato on saxophone, Dick de Pauw on violin and Bert Bassett on banjo.

Hylton was influenced by Paul Whiteman and modelled his own orchestra on Whiteman's. He concentrated his efforts on touring while occasionally appearing in London shows. By 1926, Jack Hylton and his Orchestra were well established and made their very first broadcast. They were never regular broadcasters on the BBC so their appearances on the air were greeted as occasions not to be missed; they were also the first British band to be broadcast to the United States. In the late 1930s they appeared on commercial radio's *Rinso Radio Revue* in recorded half-hour programmes. Hylton himself had the foresight to have his broadcasts recorded and stored in his archives.

Between 1927 and 1938 the band made 16 European tours and was extremely successful throughout Europe. In 1932, Hylton was awarded the French Legion of Honour for his services to music.

Jack Hylton was famous both for presenting symphonic concert arrangements and for his impressive stage effects. The band was strong vocally and included over the years such singers as Sam Browne, Pat O'Malley, Alice Mann, Denny Dennis, Hylton's sister Dolly Elsie, June Malo, Bruce Trent and Dick Murphy as well as the vocal group that Jack discovered and took to Europe – the Swingtette. Out of the Jack Hylton Band came such future bandleaders as Billy Ternent, Paul Fenoulhet, Chappie D'Amato, Jerry Hoey, Peter Yorke and Jack Jackson. His musicians were paid well in return for high standards. Hylton organised visits to Britain by Duke Ellington, Louis Armstrong and others and in 1935 he set his sights on touring the USA. He secured a contract for 13 hour-long broadcasts in the US sponsored by the Standard Oil Company. The whole band set sail on 16 October and broadcast in mid-ocean. However, due to a ban on foreign musicians by the American Musicians' Federation, only Hylton, Ternent, singers Pat O'Malley and Peggy Dell and six other performers were granted permission to work. An American band was formed under Hylton's direction to play and broadcast from the Drake Hotel in Chicago.

In 1940, because most of his musicians had joined the armed forces, Hylton disbanded and began to concentrate on his management activities. The band gave their farewell concert at the Paris Opera House. After the war, Hylton became a very successful impresario, bringing shows such as *The Crazy Gang*, *Kiss Me Kate*, *Kismet* and *Camelot* to London audiences. There were two occasions when Jack Hylton conducted again. On 12 October 1943, he conducted the Glenn Miller Orchestra in the 1936 concert arrangement of 'She Shall Have Music' which was broadcast. In 1950 he conducted a reunion Hylton Orchestra, including vocalists Sam Browne and Bruce Trent, at the Royal Command Performance. He died in 1965. It was the 1930s that saw the rise of the great British bands, such as those of Roy Fox, Ray Noble, Harry Roy, Ted Heath, and Lew Stone,

The Ted Heath Band, although less well-known in the US, was probably the first "world music" band. His music style has been characterised as a blend of Stan Kenton, Glenn Miller and Count Basie with just a small bit of British "hotel orchestra" thrown in to make the sound very smooth, very big and very impressive. Bandleaders and music critics in the US considered Heath's band to be precise, polished and professional. From its inception in 1945, the band showcased the best musicians in Britain. Heath sought out the best musicians he could find and made sure the band always presented a superior professional appearance and played flawlessly.

Above: Jack Hylton and his band – giant of the British music scene for four decades.

Above: Precise, polished and professional – Ted Heath.

BIOGRAPHY:

Edward "Ted" Heath

Born 30 March 1902 in Wandsworth, London
Theme song: 'Listen to My Music'

Ted Heath's father taught him tenor horn at six years old, and at eight he was playing in local brass band contests. At 14 he switched to trombone. In 1919, Ted's father fell ill and Ted had to play in street bands ("busking") for money to support the family. In the early 1920s, he rashly accepted a job playing with Jack Hylton's dance band at the popular London venue, the Queen's Hall Roof Gardens. After only four days he was ordered to go home and practice some more.

His first real band gig was with an American band on tour in Europe – the Southern Syncopation Orchestra – which had an engagement in Vienna, Austria, and needed a trombone player. The drummer for this band, Benny Payton, taught Ted all about jazz and swing. Ted had to pay his own way back from Austria when the band ran out of money.

He next played with the Metro-Gnomes, a small band fronted by Ennis Parkes, who later became Mrs Jack Hylton. In late 1920, he again joined the Jack Hylton theatre band. From 1925 to 1926 Ted played in the Kit-Cat Club's band led by American Al Starita. There he heard Bunny Berigan, the Dorseys and Paul Whiteman when they toured Europe.

In 1928, he joined Bert Ambrose's orchestra at the Mayfair Hotel in London and played there until 1935. Next he moved on to Sydney Lipton's orchestra at the Grosvenor House. Ambrose, a strict disciplinarian, taught Ted how to be a bandleader. It was during this time that he became a master of his instrument and swing music.

In September 1939 the war caused an immediate disbandment of the Sydney Lipton Band which was on tour in Scotland at the time. Heath and his family made their way back to London where, in late 1939, he joined Maurice Winnick's Dorchester Hotel band. During the late 1930s and early 1940s, he played as a sideman on several Benny Carter albums.

In 1940, Heath joined Geraldo's Orchestra and played hundreds of concerts and broadcasts during the war. He often became one of the "boys" in Geraldo's vocal group, Three Boys and a Girl. In 1941, Geraldo asked his band members to submit a favourite tune to include in their broadcasts. Heath composed two songs, 'Gonna Love That Guy' and 'That Lovely Weekend', with his wife Moira, who wrote the lyrics. It was the latter song that Heath gave to Geraldo – at which point it was orchestrated with Dorothy Carless on vocals, becoming an instant hit. The royalties from these two songs allowed Heath to form his own band.

In 1944, Douglas Lawrence, the Dance Music Organiser for the BBC's Variety Department, was talked into giving Heath's new band a broadcasting contract. At first Lawrence was sceptical as Heath wanted to implement a bigger band than anyone had seen before. In 1944 the Ted Heath Band made their first BBC broadcast. At first they only played radio dates, and the same year Heath was given his own regular radio show. Sometime during this period, Ted heard the great Glenn Miller Army Air Force Band and was completely taken with their sound. In 1945, the BBC decreed that only permanent, touring bands could appear on radio and so on D-Day the permanent Ted Heath Band was officially formed.

In late 1945, Tootie Camarata, American bandleader and trumpet player, came to UK as musical director for the film *London Town* and commissioned Heath to provide the music for the film. The money from this allowed the band to stay alive although the film itself was unsuccessful. In 1946, Heath arranged a stint at the Winter Gardens in Blackpool, a Scandinavian tour, a fortnight at the London Casino with Lena Horne, and also backed Ella Fitzgerald at the London

Palladium. All told they played 109 of the Palladium's alternating "Sunday Swing Sessions" which lasted until August 1955. The band played three Royal Variety Performances – in 1948, 1949 and 1951.

In 1956 Heath went on his first US tour, with the assistance of the Sir Edward Lewis of Decca Records, the British Musicians' Union and Stan Kenton, the US bandleader. An exchange agreement was made between Ted Heath and Kenton, whereby Kenton would tour Britain at the same time Ted Heath toured the US. Also included in the deal were the services of Nat King Cole, June Christy and the Four Freshmen. Heath's band performed 43 concerts in 30 cities, primarily in the southern states, over 31 days. During the tour, Nat Cole was hit in the mouth on stage in Birmingham, Alabama, by a group of white segregationists who jumped up out of the audience. Because of this Heath nearly cancelled the rest of the tour.

On 1 May 1956, 7,000 miles later, they gave their final US performance at Carnegie Hall. On the way, the band's instrument truck was delayed by bad weather. Their instruments finally arrived just minutes before the curtains were raised and so the band had no time to warm up or rehearse. They went on stage "cold". They needn't have worried; there were so many encore calls that Nat Cole, who was backstage, but not on the bill, had to come out on stage and ask people to leave.

For over 25 years, the band retained its personnel nearly intact and held a reunion in 1966 to mark its 21st anniversary. At that time, many of the original band members were still playing with the band. Heath usually played with four to five trumpets, four to five trombones, five reeds, drums, bass and piano, along with the occasional use of guitar, vibes and tuba. During the band's career they recorded over 100 45rpm records and albums, covering more than 800 different song titles, nearly all of which were uniquely arranged for the prodigious talents of this band as Heath never played "stock" arrangements. Up until December 2000, the Ted Heath Band was still playing limited gigs in and around London with many of the original band members, now led by long-time trombone player Don Lusher, a bandleader in his own right. However, due to the advancing age of its members and the difficulty of finding musicians who were capable of playing the demanding tunes, the Heath family decided to disband the group. On 4 December 2000 the band, many of whom were original members, played their farewell concert at the Royal Festival Hall in London.

Ted Heath had died on 18 November 1969.

"Music and dancing (the more the pity) have become so closely associated with ideas of riot and debauchery among the less cultivated classes, that a taste for them, for their own sakes, can hardly be said to exist, and before they can be recommended as innocent or safe amusements, a very great change of ideas must take place."

SIR JOHN HERSCHEL

Other British bands played an important part in the big band era. For example, the top bands of 1940 included:

Eddie Carroll Orchestra, Geraldo and his Orchestra, Carroll Gibbons Orchestra, Henry Hall Orchestra, Jack Harris Orchestra, Jack Jackson Orchestra, Ken Jones Orchestra, Sydney Lipton Orchestra, Joe Loss Orchestra, Mantovani Orchestra, Oscar Rabin Orchestra, Harry Roy Orchestra, Billy Ternent Orchestra and the Maurice Winnick Orchestra.

The most popular British vocalists in the 1940s were:

Al Bowlly, Sam Browne, Jack Cooper, Sam Costa, Evelyn Dahl, Beryl Davis, Denny Dennis, Dan Donovan, Leslie Douglas, Dolly Elsie, Gracie Fields, Chick Henderson, Anne Lenner, Celia Lipton, Vera Lynn and Anne Shelton.

Finally, it is again worth emphasising that the great engine driving the music and the bands was ballroom dancing (this was true the world over, not just in Britain). Music and dancing combined to form a way of life. It should probably be noted that meeting people was the prime motivation for dancing. Perhaps half of the young men at a dance were there to meet a young lady. Conversely, half of the young ladies were there to meet a nice young man looking for a nice young lady.

In addition to the dance halls found in major cities, there were thousands of weekend dances held in suburban areas – usually at a local church. The music consisted of anything from phonograph records to trios and even small home-town bands. While a donation of one shilling could get you into the local church dance, five shillings was the entry price for such posh London venues as the Trocadero, the Astoria Ballroom, the Hammersmith Palais, the Lyceum and many others (where many of the patrons were expert dancers).

During World War II, many venues had to be closed due to wartime restrictions. Still many bands managed to hang on (with inferior sidemen, as a rule), and of course the music – especially the music that carried memories of home and the girl left behind – went with the fighting men overseas. Many of the bandsmen who were inducted into the armed forces managed to stay together in regimental bands and such, playing in such unlikely places as aircraft hangars and deckside on ships.

The British government supported an organisation called CEMA, which provided funds to small musical groups, symphony orchestras and theatre companies (including the Old Vic theatre group that toured the provinces). However one man, Ernest Bevin, believed that CEMA's operas and classical music were not necessarily appropriate for the workers in Britain's wartime factories, and he convinced government to support his ENSA – the Entertainments National Service Association. ENSA sent popular music entertainers into factories and service bases where workers and servicemen greeted them enthusiastically.

At the same time the armed forces bands began to move away from strictly military music to play at dance halls themselves

One of the most popular of these was the Squadronaires, who made a surprising return to the public eye long after the war had ended. And another British band whose main success came in the post-war years was that of Billy Cotton.

Above: The great engine driving the music and the bands was ballroom dancing.

BIOGRAPHY:
Billy Cotton

Born 6 May 1899 in Westminster, London
Theme song: 'Somebody Stole My Gal"

Billy Cotton was the youngest in a family of 10 children. As a boy he sang solo treble in St Margaret's Church choir. He learned to play the drums whilst he was enlisted during World War I as a bugler/drummer and was in active service during the Dardanelles campaign in Gallipoli. Later in the war he served in the Royal Flying Corps.

After the war Cotton worked as a bus driver in London. During the 1920s he began a successful sporting career, first playing for Brentford football club and then in the 1930s representing Britain as a racing driver for the ERA team. He continued with his musical interests throughout by playing drums for various bands. In 1924, whilst with the Laurie Johnson Band, he played the British Empire Exhibition at Wembley. He then went on to form the London Savannah Band which he fronted and which featured the pianist and arranger Clem Bernard. Their partnership would last for over 40 years. At first they played the large dance halls, until in 1928 they received their big break at the London Astoria. The Cotton band also played in the top nightclubs of the day, for example Ciro's, in both London and Paris.

In the 1930s they moved into cine-variety with their first film appearance in 1934 in a film entitled *The First Mrs Fraser*. They then became a theatre showband following the introduction of a more saucy repertoire of songs and broad visual humour. Band personnel during

the 1930s included Jack Doyle, Alan Breeze, Nat Gonella, Teddy Foster and Ellis Jackson, the American tapdancer and trombonist.

Throughout World War II, Cotton entertained the troops in France with ENSA. He was put in charge of the Air Training Corps because of his service during World War I. He also toured the music halls.

After the war the band's variety bookings took a downturn but in 1949 Cotton was given *Wakey, Wakey!!*, a Sunday afternoon radio programme on the BBC which was to run for over 20 years, becoming a national institution. Tunes such as 'Maybe It's Because I'm a Londoner' and his theme song 'Somebody Stole My Gal' were all performed by regular personnel such as Johnny Johnson, Doreen Stevens, Kathy Kaye, Rita Williams and the Highlights.

In 1953, the year of the Queen's coronation, he scored a hit with the song 'In A Golden Coach'. Further hits of the 1950s included 'Friends and Neighbours', 'I Saw Mommy Kissing Santa Claus' and 'Puttin' On the Style'. In 1957 *The Billy Cotton Band Show* was aired on BBC television for the first of hundreds of appearances in which Cotton danced with the chorus girls, known as the Silhouettes, and swapped banter with Max Bygraves, the pianist Russ Conway and singer Alma Cogan. Billy

Above: Billy Cotton and his band.

Cotton's son Billy Cotton Junior, was by this time a producer of light entertainment for the BBC and was often at the production helm for the show.

In 1962 Billy Cotton was voted Show Business Personality of the Year. He continued working throughout the 1960s until his death on 25 March 1969. Cotton was buried at St Margaret's Church, where he had first started in music as a choirboy.

Above: Billy Cotton, voted Show Business Personality of the Year in 1962.

BIOGRAPHY:

The Squadronaires

The Squadronaires were formed during World War II and, as the name suggests, consisted of members of the RAF – but these servicemen had previously been sidemen of Bert Ambrose's band.

For most of the war up to 1945, the line-up consisted of:
Tommy McQuater, Archie Craig and Clinton French on trumpets; George Chisholm and Eric Breeze on trombones; Tommy Bradbury, Harry Lewis (Vera Lynn's husband), Jimmy Durrant, Andy McDevitt, Cliff Townshend (father of Peter Townshend of the Who) on saxophone; Ronnie Aldrich on piano; Sid Colin on guitar; Arthur Maden (who was also the band's manager) on bass; Jock Cummings on drums and Jimmy Miller on vocals also acting as bandleader.

In 1945, Jimmy Watson (trumpet) replaced Clinton "Froggy" French while Monty Levy, on alto saxophone, replaced Harry Lewis. The band continued with occasional personnel changes and in 1950 Ronnie Aldrich, an arranger, took over as leader. The band was renamed Ronnie Aldrich and the Squadronaires and the line-up was:

Ron Simmonds, Gracie Cole and Archie Craig on trumpets; Ric Kennedy and Bill Geldard on trombones; Cliff Townshend, Monty Levy, Andy McDevitt, Cyril Reubens and Ken Kiddier on saxophones; Don Innes on piano; Andy Reveley on bass; Tommy Cairns on drums; Roy Edwards and Andy Reveley on vocals.

Later on Gracie Cole and her husband Bill Geldard were replaced by Terry Lewis on trumpet and Johnny Keating on trombone. The Squadronaires disbanded in 1964. But that was not the end of the story.

In 1987 the band was revived by Harry Bence who had been a member of another RAF wartime band, the Fourth Barrage Balloon Band. He had also worked with a number of post-war British dance bands including those of Ken MacIntosh, Joe Loss, Eric Winstone and Ted Heath. Under Bence The New Squadronaires made several albums. Included were *Flying Home*, *Big Band Spectacular* and in 1992 the appropriately named *Something in the Air*.

Above: The Squadronaires.

THE BEAT GOES ON

World War II also played its part in diminishing the interest in big bands. Bands lost many of their best musicians to the draft and many of those lost their lives in action. Fuel rationing also meant that band tours were next to impossible.

In the United States, the Musicians' Union went on a recording strike that began on 1 August 1942. No agreement was reached until September 1943 when Decca made the first concessions. Blue Note followed in November 1943, and other independent labels signed on later that year. Columbia and Victor, however did not settle until November 1944. Because most of swing's top performers were signed to either Columbia or Victor, many went for more than two years without making any recordings. Singers, on the other hand, were not part of the union, and thus they could carry on recording. Singers increased in popularity and came to overshadow the big bands. Most of the bands on the labels which agreed with the union early on were not swing bands, but they quickly gained followings by having new records available.

In 1941, a cabaret tax was enacted in the USA which meant clubs had to pay 30% of their ticket sales in taxes. This resulted in the clubs hiring cheaper and smaller bands and so many of the swing-playing big bands lost out.

However, New Orleans jazz – Dixieland – experienced a resurgence in popularity. Also another form of jazz was growing, called bebop, which was more about listening than dancing (and indeed was difficult to dance to). Then there was rhythm and blues, whose bands were less expensive to maintain, and had a new sound. These changes in music attracted band members away from swing, as well as the listeners. Finally, with the end of the war, people did not want to be reminded of that time. Swing, so popular when the war started,

came to be seen as a reminder of those years of suffering, anger and loss of loved ones. People simply shelved their swing 78s and found new music to help them forget. The swing era was dead – temporarily.

From the 1950s up until the early 1960s, every American teenager knew how to dance what would later be known as East Coast Swing. Then Chubby Checker's 'The Twist' killed off partner, or "touch", dancing.

THE NEO-SWING ERA

Swing, where the music is indivisible from the dance, simply wouldn't stay dead. In recent years a new swing revival has been taking place all over the world. Emerging from a 50-year break, swing is once again king, and the joints are jumpin' around the globe, hopping in New York and even doing the salsa in Manchester. East Coast Swing, both the original ballroom version and the looser street version, are being taught to new dancers. West Coast Swing is popular in a number of clubs in Southern California.

To the current generation, weaned on dancing with a volume so pumped-up that all conversation is shut out; and with partners kept at arm's length or farther, the social aspects of swing's upbeat, infectious rhythm and casual physical contact have proved particularly appealing. Many of today's new "swingsters", bored with the old formless, free-style dancing of techno and hip-hop clubs, like being able to grab on to their partners.

They're dancing not only to the music of Benny Goodman and Louis Jordan, but also to the jump-jiving, faster-paced retro bands such as Big Bad VooDoo Daddy, who appeared in the recent *Swingers* film, the Flying Newtrinos, the Squirrel Nut Zippers and the Flipped Fedoras, with their modern, updated, and somewhat faster-paced take on big-band-era music. Now there is a tinge of ska or hip-hop in some of the new music, bringing a new angle to swing. Brian Setzer with his rockabilly background is taking on old classics in a big-band style. Louis Prima – the man who wrote 'Sing, Sing, Sing', the tune popularised by Benny Goodman – who also continued his career into the

1950s with many comedic tunes, is seemingly well known by almost any modern Lindy Hopper.

Frankie Manning, the man credited with creating the first aerial in Lindy Hop, went on to perform with Whitey's Lindy Hoppers in several movies, and later with his own dance troupe the Congoroos. In the early 1980s, he was approached by a number of people including the Rhythm Hot Shots from Sweden and dance partners Erin Stevens and Steven Mitchell. They urged him out of retirement to teach people how to dance the Lindy Hop the way he remembered it from the days of the Savoy Ballroom.

Many dance schools are reporting a surge in numbers of students learning the classic swing dance. It appears that swing and the Lindy Hop, born in Harlem 70 years ago, are here to stay.

At clubs, ballrooms, and school dances, you will find the dance of swing offers a joyous escape for a generation that came of age during the AIDS crisis, and a time when sexuality was hidden under grunge. This is a return to elegance, to "touch" dancing and to wearing your sexuality on your sleeve. It's an open rebellion against the grunge music era of the early 1990s and the clinical computerised dance music played in many clubs today.

In 2001 Robbie Williams released his *Swing When You're Winning* album, a masterful tribute to the Anglo-American big-band swing revival. In December 2001 Williams, alongside a 58-piece big band and special guests, gave a live performance at the Royal Albert Hall.

Now swing really is the thing!

PLAYLIST

Just ten pieces of music and songs which evoke the era of big bands, jazz and swing:

TITLE	ARTIST
SING, SING, SING	BENNY GOODMAN
BIG NOISE FROM WINETKA	GENE KRUPA
ON THE SUNNY SIDE OF THE STREET	LOUIS ARMSTRONG
TAKE THE "A" TRAIN	DUKE ELLINGTON
MINNIE THE MOOCHER	CAB CALLOWAY
ONE O'CLOCK JUMP	COUNT BASIE
IN THE MOOD	GLENN MILLER
THE BREEZE AND I	JIMMY DORSEY
SPECIAL DELIVERY STOMP	ARTIE SHAW
EL MANICERO	XAVIER CUGAT

INDEX